# TRAVELS IN AMERICAN IRAQ

# TRAVELS IN AMERICAN IRAQ

## JOHN MARTINKUS

Black Inc.

Published by Black Inc.
An imprint of Schwartz Publishing

Level 5, 289 Flinders Lane
Melbourne Victoria 3000 Australia
email: enquiries@blackincbooks.com
http://www.blackincbooks.com

National Library of Australia Cataloguing-in-Publication entry:

    Martinkus, John.
    Travels in American Iraq.

    ISBN 1 86395 285 3.

    1. Iraq War, 2003. 2. Iraq - Military relations - United
    States. 3. United States - Military relations - Iraq. I.
    Title.

    956.70443

Book design: Thomas Deverall

Printed in Australia by Griffin Press

# CONTENTS

WELCOME TO AMERICAN IRAQ             7

FALLUJA                            24

SIGNS OF TORTURE                   44

KARBALA                            51

AFTERMATH                          72

DEMOCRACY IN THE MAKING            91

ABU GHRAIB                        101

LAST STOP ON THE ORIENT EXPRESS   115

BASRA                             126

ONE YEAR ON                       153

GREATER KURDISTAN                 170

LAST DAYS                         192

2 March 2004: *I reached the bomb scene not more than a minute after the explosion. The flood of people escaping the first blast had swept past, forcing me to take cover behind a pillar. The only ones left were those who had been caught in the explosion, and they were lying on the ground injured. I'd felt the heat from the explosion on my face. The panicked crowd had run the other way and suddenly the road was clear, so I simply walked over to where the bomb had gone off. Pieces of bodies lay all around the intersection. In the middle of the road one man sat upright, even though his body seemed to have split down the side like a ripped seam. Blood poured from his sides and his head onto the road. He was still alive but dying in front of me. It was suddenly quiet and there was no one near, just that man along with bodies and parts of bodies and another man lying on the ground with his legs kicking in a reflex action who – I think – was already dead. I saw what was a severed small child's hand, half-shredded and wet, lying on the blood-covered road. There was no sign of the rest of the body. I was shaking and trying to hold my camera still. Under my foot I felt something slippery and my heel skidded. When I looked down, what I saw was unmistakable. It was part of a human brain. I gagged and my eyes filled with water as I tried to steady the camera and not throw up.*

*Two weeks earlier:*

It was pitch black and bitterly cold when we reached the border. The lights were out in the Jordanian customs house, and we waited in the large, low-roofed building in the dark, surrounded by Iraqis and Jordanians pushing and shoving and demanding to know what the hold-up was. The officials behind the counter occasionally lit a cigarette lighter just so we knew they were still there. I never found out why the power was off. Maybe it was a malfunction or maybe a security precaution, but pretty soon we heard a generator start outside and a few neon tubes flickered back to life.

The owner of the vehicle we had rented in Amman had told us we must leave the Jordanian capital at midnight in order to cross the Jordan–Iraq border at first light. The aim was to reach Baghdad by the middle of the day, thereby passing the towns of Ramadi and Falluja early in the morning when, he assured us, there would be no attacks on traffic.

He had not lost a car yet, he said proudly, as he poured whiskies for me and my companion, Australian photographer Steve Dupont, while we waited in his office in Amman. He was used to dealing with journalists. He ran a hotel that had once catered to tourists, but of course there were not so many of them anymore so instead he dealt mainly with reporters, NGO workers and human rights activists. As his cars to Baghdad were among the cheapest available, he was used to dealing with the lower end of the market. During the war in

2003 this had mostly comprised freelancers and human shields. By early 2004 there was still a steady stream of activists and journalists making the trip to Baghdad who were unable to pay the prices asked by Royal Jordanian Airlines, which ran the only commercial service to the Iraqi capital.

In his office he had pointed proudly to a stuffed white wolf that sat upon his bookshelf. It had been looted from one of Saddam's palaces and given to him by an English journalist as he passed back through Jordan after last year's war. Its mouth was still open in a snarl. The taxidermist who worked for Saddam had preserved the tongue and teeth beautifully, but unfortunately the legs were broken and pointed forward. It looked like it had been stuffed in a bag at some stage in its afterlife.

Melodramatically our host pulled out two large spent shells and placed them on the desk in front of him. Steve and I sipped our whisky as he said, 'Gentlemen, these bullets are worth less than a dollar each. No story is worth your life.' I wondered how many times he had produced the two shells and said that. He proceeded to tell us that the Iraqis were a tough people and they could tell when you were not honest with them.

Steve and I had both flown in from Australia the day before. We had left on a lazy mid-February Saturday afternoon when the temperature was in the low forties and Australia still seemed to be on holiday after the Christmas break. In Jordan it was snowing. At midnight, when we finally headed off into the desert, we covered ourselves in blankets and both immediately fell asleep in the car. We were still too exhausted from the twenty-hour flight and the time difference to worry much about where we were going.

Once the lights were turned on in the customs house, things proceeded relatively quickly and we crossed over to the Iraqi side. A tired man stamped a visa with no end date and no conditions into our passport and we were through. It was one of the smoothest border crossings I had experienced anywhere in the world – no searches, no questions and no payments required. Aside from one cold-looking Iraqi guard with a solitary AK47 there was no sign of any authority, just the smashed-up buildings on the Iraqi side with no windows, and an arch across the road which had once said something but from which the writing had long since been erased.

The highway led straight east through the desert, and our driver accelerated to 140 kilometres an hour as the sun started to come up over the horizon in front of us. Steve passed me a bottle of Cuban rum and said, 'Welcome to Iraq.' To one side two Humvees sat stationary in the desert, with two soldiers on top bundled up against the cold manning .50 calibre guns. They were the only Coalition troops we saw for the next four hours.

It wasn't until we reached the outskirts of Falluja that there was any sign of trouble. The traffic was mainly trucks carrying containers and second-hand cars from as far away as Germany, and white and orange taxis full of people travelling from Jordan to Baghdad. All the cars drove at well over a hundred and nobody stopped for the occasional broken-down taxi on the side of the road. There was the odd wrecked vehicle and downed power lines, as well as crushed sections of metal barriers which I later learned were the result of tanks crossing over to the other lanes of the highway. Generally, though, it looked like a highway through a desert anywhere in the world.

As we neared Falluja, I saw ahead of us a group of men waving down cars with AK47s. Our car slowed, and what turned out to be Iraqi police, wearing leather jackets stretched tightly over body armour, yelled at the driver to pull over. The driver shouted to him that we were journalists, and the policeman, wide-eyed with stress and fear, yelled at us to keep moving while simultaneously waving his gun at another vehicle to stop. Lines of cars had been halted and they were parked along the side of the road as more police ran up and down checking the occupants. As they did this, they shouted at each other and at the people in the cars while still more policemen stood on a nearby embankment with their weapons trained on the vehicles.

Two days before, on 14 February, the police in Falluja had been attacked in their police station in the town, and seventeen of them killed and thirty-seven wounded in a gun battle that lasted for three hours. The insurgents sealed off roads in the town with their own roadblocks and proceeded to lay siege to the police station.

In the ensuing battle the police, armed only with assault rifles and light machine-guns, were overpowered by their attackers, who were equipped with RPGs and mortars. The battle only ended when all of the several dozen prisoners inside the police station were released as the insurgents broke into the jail.

Falluja is only an hour's drive west of Baghdad, and after we had passed through the dusty, flat town we started to encounter long convoys of US military vehicles. They were in the process of carrying out the largest troop rotation of US forces since World War II. It amounted to the movement of 240,000 personnel: 130,000 outgoing and 110,000 incoming. The rotation of troops in the Falluja area would have disastrous results for that town, but on my first day in Iraq the sight of so many Coalition troops on the move inspired in me a feeling of security. The place seemed firmly under control.

# WELCOME TO AMERICAN IRAQ

The highway led straight into the centre of Baghdad, and almost before we knew it we were in the chaotic traffic of the downtown area. A large chunk of central Baghdad had been sealed off in the 'Green Zone', a 10-kilometre-square area where the US civil and military administration resided, and this meant negotiating the rest of the downtown where Coalition roadblocks moved and changed on a daily basis. Bridges, roads and freeways were routinely blocked for hours on end with no explanation or notice given while civilian vehicles submitted to endless re-routing, traffic jams and countless vehicle checks by US soldiers, Iraqi police or Iraqi Civil Defense Corps (ICDC) troops. Our Jordanian driver, who had been driving for almost twelve hours non-stop, quickly got lost. He tried to distract us from this fact by pointing out the buildings that had been blown up recently in the wave of bombings that began in the second half of 2003.

We got stuck in traffic in a backstreet that was half blocked off by the razor wire coils of a building important enough to consider itself a target. A young man came racing out of the crowd being chased by some people and jumped on the front bonnet of a car inching its way in the opposite direction down the jammed street. He started kicking outwards at his pursuers, who had surrounded the car and were now trying to grab at his legs. Another man arrived, yelling and waving a pistol. There was a lot of shouting and the pistol was aimed at the young man who then jumped off the bonnet. The crowd followed and grabbed him. Our Jordanian driver was muttering to himself and sweating profusely as he drove aggressively through the traffic.

He pulled up finally in Sadoun Street, the main street of Baghdad where the major hotels are located. He pointed to the razor wire and concrete blast walls that blocked the sidewalk on the opposite side of the road and jumped out and began unloading our bags. Steve's blond hair, sunglasses and camera bags brought stares from passing cars as we tried to cross the busy street. By the time we made it across, the Jordanian was already gone. Before us were the Kurdish guards, razor wire and sandbagged machine-gun emplacement that blocked the gate to the Hotel Baghdad.

Steve tried to explain to the guards that he was on assignment for a magazine that had arranged for him to stay at the Baghdad. He was working with a writer profiling an American policeman who was training the

Iraqi police. As the policeman lived at the Baghdad, it made sense for Steve to stay there. What we didn't know was that the Baghdad was widely believed to be the hotel of choice for the CIA, and the Kurdish guards – chosen for their loyalty to their US employers – were under strict orders that no one was to enter.

It took a while to sort it all out. There were lots of shouted commands and everybody seemed to be armed with at least one weapon and to be wearing body armour. The guards insisted on emptying our bags onto the table. Eventually a short Asian security woman with an American accent and an AK47 came to the checkpoint with a two-way radio and called through to the office. It was okay, they were expecting Steve. He was given clearance to enter and so, by default, so was I. It was difficult, she said, as she escorted us behind the blast barriers, they had been hit by a car bomb in October, and in consequence there were now strict entry rules. There were also language problems with the guards. The fact that there were two of us, and we were unannounced and had come straight to the gate carrying large bags, had convinced the Kurds that there was something suspicious about us. No one was allowed in from the street unless they were escorted and held a Coalition weapons permit. Another thing that had excited suspicion was our lack of large weapons.

We walked through a small shopping mall that occupied the courtyard in front of the Baghdad. The mall was now a series of wrecked shopfronts with no windows and broken bits of ceiling hanging down in the empty shops. A barber's chair sat among the debris in one shop and others showed signs of fire damage. It was here that the car bomb had gone off in October. There had been two suicide bombers. Security had managed to shoot dead the first driver before he managed to explode himself and his car; the second had then let off his device prematurely. Since that time the entire area in front of the hotel had been barricaded and the street could no longer be seen. The sidewalk in one of Baghdad's busiest shopping strips was now off-limits to anyone but authorised personnel.

The Baghdad itself was just a simple '60s tower block about six storeys high. It backed onto the river and was surrounded on all sides by concrete blast walls and razor wire barricades. These were spaced well away from the hotel to provide protection against VBIEDS or 'vehicle-borne improvised explosive devices' – car bombs. Everyone outside the hotel but inside the cordon was armed, and on the roof could be seen several sandbagged positions with weapons trained on the streets below. The Asian contractor handed us over to the guard in the foyer and then relayed that information to someone on her two-way radio. The next guard walked us up the stairs into the hotel lobby and handed us in turn to a young Australian in her mid-twenties who carried a handgun and introduced herself as Louisa.

Louisa ran through the amenities of the hotel like a well-rehearsed concierge. The spiel seemed out of place in a foyer where the dated lounge chairs were occupied either by middle-aged, overweight men wearing body armour and cradling automatic weapons, or by young American soldiers wearing helmets and body armour and resting their combat boots on the small tables. Some of the younger soldiers were smoking large cigars. Steve remarked on the security and Louisa replied without batting an eyelid that they were very proud of it – it was the best in Baghdad. She worked for DynCorp, the company that now ran the hotel, and was subcontracted to train the Iraqi police force. Most of DynCorp's employees were former US police, which explained the preponderance of moustaches and massive beer guts straining out from underneath armour.

The hotel was one of the few places outside the sealed-off Green Zone where it was safe for Iraqis who worked with the Coalition Provisional Authority to eat and stay when they were in Baghdad. The Iraqi civilians who were wandering around the lobby or eating in the dining room were high-profile targets of the insurgents, so the extravagant security precautions and the presence of heavily armed personnel equipped with two-way radios began to make sense.

DynCorp employees themselves were as much a target as the Iraqi politicians of the Governing Council. The company was given the contract to provide 1000 ex-US police or prison officers for 'law enforcement support' for Iraq when the war officially ended on 1 May 2003. The initial contract was worth US$50 million for the first year but it had increased in 2004 with more personnel deployed and DynCorp picking up more subcontracting work in facilitating the rehabilitation of Iraq's telephone network. To get a job on the Iraq mission the applicant needed to have between five and eight years' experience as a United States police or corrections officer, have an American passport, be in good health, and be able to use a 9mm semi-automatic handgun. Experience in US border control was also acceptable, which was fortunate as DynCorp itself runs this operation.

DynCorp has run missions like the one in Iraq in Haiti, Kosovo, Bosnia and Central America. It employs 25,000 people and has an annual income of two billion American dollars. In 2002 DynCorp employees in Bosnia were accused of sex-slave trading involving girls as young as twelve. A British employee who complained of the practice was sacked for discrediting the company and the company was later ordered to pay £100,000 by a British court for unfair dismissal. In 2001 Ecuadorian peasants brought a class action against DynCorp in the US courts for spraying defoliant chemicals on their homes and farms, destroying their livelihood and causing illness and the death of children. DynCorp aircraft and personnel were also engaged in anti-narcotic operations to wipe out the cocaine production in neighbouring Colombia, which is one of its US government contracts. More and more, companies like DynCorp perform tasks traditionally carried out by the US military.

The utilisation of such companies is constantly criticised because of their lack of accountability – but this is often the very reason they were contracted in the first place.

The company has long been accused of being a front for CIA activities and operatives. In late 2001, DynCorp was contracted by the CIA to carry out tasks including the protection of Afghan President Hamid Karzai (the US State Department later assumed this responsibility in November 2002). When the car bomb went off outside the Hotel Baghdad in December 2003, both al-Jazeera and al-Arabiya television identified the building as the Baghdad CIA headquarters, which wasn't very far from the truth.

*

After the long drive to get there, the atmosphere inside the Baghdad was a little stifling. People stared, and every time Steve and I moved around the hotel we would be asked us what we were doing. Deciding to go for a walk, we were told there was only one direction we could go, along the Tigris River at the back of the hotel to the adjoining security zone of the Palestine and Sheraton hotels.

Exiting the Hotel Baghdad compound was no easy task. At the back gate, coils of razor wire blocked the entrance and there was a sandbagged guard post. Luckily an American policeman – a New Yorker – I had known in East Timor was at the rear gate. At first he failed to recognise me, as I now had a beard. He told me he had been in Iraq since April 2003. He looked terrible: red in the face, worn-out and constantly twitching. As he talked, he yelled orders at the Kurds and the other DynCorp staff securing the gate. He was very tense and jumpy and the two-way radio strapped to his chest kept issuing queries and orders. His job was to oversee the compound's security and to contend with the constant threats or perceived threats against DynCorp staff and their charges.

In East Timor, I recalled, he cursed the fact that he had been sent on a mission without a weapon, particularly after an unarmed American policeman had been shot by the Indonesians. Here he was carrying a huge automatic rifle with a grenade launcher attached to it. He told me how he and his colleagues had acquired these. As the US State Department placed restrictions on the importation of weapons, the DynCorp arsenal had been acquired mostly from markets in Baghdad or from confiscations by the police or the military. There was no shortage of military-issue weapons in Baghdad, and anything from the heavy machine-guns in the sandbagged posts to Uzi 9mm machine pistols, grenade launchers (RPGs) and pistols were freely available. Almost everybody in the compound carried an AK47 rifle.

Outside the compound there was no sense of normality. The side roads had been blocked by concrete barriers and razor wire. There was no traffic and the only Iraqis present were either armed guards or translators.

The shops and houses were empty and boarded-up. Guards at each checkpoint followed our progress as we walked. Beyond the checkpoints, concrete barriers more than fifteen feet high provided a shield for traffic and pedestrians who had passed through the checkpoint on the way to their hotel. The barriers were positioned to block shots from the apartment block on the other side of Sadoun Street. Once you had passed through the checkpoint, you could only be going to the Palestine or the Sheraton and then you were fair game for the insurgents. Later I read several briefs on the US casualty lists of soldiers 'shot dead on guard duty at the Palestine Hotel'.

Two massive M1A1 Abrams tanks sat parked outside the Palestine, but they looked like they had been there a long time. The hotel itself was just a mid-sized tower block, with a chintzy foyer full of middle-aged businessmen wearing body armour over their business shirts or hanging over their shoulders. A tall American with a white cowboy hat and a long raincoat stalked around the foyer talking loudly into one of the Thuraya hand-held satellite phones that I later discovered hardly ever get a clear signal. It was business as usual of sorts, with a DHL counter in the corner of the foyer offering next-day delivery to Europe and America, a newspaper stand selling last week's magazines, yesterday's Jordanian papers and the *International Herald Tribune*. Iraqi men in suits talked quietly in groups in the armchairs in the foyer, and the bored-looking staff stood behind the service desk laughing at private jokes. Western men in casual civilian clothes and carrying AK47s strolled into the foyer and headed for the lifts while ripping off the Velcro flaps holding their armour in place.

Many of these people had been placed under security restrictions by their companies and organisations and were not allowed to leave the secure zone without their body armour or a guard. Most business was carried out in their rooms or on short trips outside. You could find most of the big-business or big-media representatives somewhere in the Palestine and the Sheraton. There wasn't anywhere else for them to go. Most of the other hotels were judged too insecure to stay in by their security consultants. Thankfully we didn't stay long. I had to leave and get a lift to the house in the suburbs where I was going to be staying.

*

Mohammed was one of the best drivers. He usually worked for *Time* magazine, which rented the house where I was staying in Baghdad. We were driving into town past a shattered telecommunications tower once known as 'Saddam Tower'. A missile had blown apart the revolving restaurant at the top in the first days of the war in 2003. The adjoining building was the Maoune communication centre; it too had been hit by one of the massive JDAM bombs intended to knock out the regime's communications. I could see clearly how the bomb had penetrated the building and punched a hole in the centre of each floor before exploding in the basement, blowing out all of the buildings' walls and windows while leaving the frame intact. I marvelled at how such a devastating bomb could be so accurate that the houses across the road appeared completely undamaged by the attack.

Mohammed wasn't interested. He drove past the old tower every day, and he was listening intently to the BBC in Arabic on the car radio. He told me a bomb had gone off that morning in front of the Polish base in Hilla: 'Eleven Iraqi civilians killed, forty-four injured, five Polish injured and maybe one US soldier. That is a big bomb.' I asked him how far it was by road. He said less than an hour. 'But we won't see anything by the time we get there. They'll clean it up,' he said. It was my first day working and I wanted to get a story. I asked him again if we should go. 'Don't worry, it is not a big story,' he said, and kept driving into town.

We pulled up at Assassins' Gate, once the main entrance to Saddam's former Republican Guard Palace, and now the main gate to the Green Zone. There had been a bombing there too, on 18 January 2004, as people lined up trying to get to work inside the zone had been blown up at eight in the morning. Twenty had died and sixty had been injured. Security was now tight, and Mohammed parked across the street. A crowd of people was forming up at the intersection in front of the main gate. The people there were Shiites, dressed in black and mostly women. They carried banners and stopped the traffic in the middle of the road. One woman, Mossun Hatab, pushed forward and started yelling at me, with Mohammed translating: 'We want land to build homes. We are poor families. We are living under the bridges,' she said. The crowd of women pushed around us and more of them started to speak. 'Some of them are living in an old military camp after the war and now they have to leave,' said Mohammed. The pushing and shouting were getting more intense and he said we should go. There was no one coming out to listen to them and they seemed to be venting their frustrations on us, the only people who had taken any notice. The US soldiers in the towers across the road had instructed them to keep on the other side of the road through their loudspeakers. The demonstration was nothing, Mohammed said as we walked away, it happened every day.

Back at the *Time* house, a Russian photographer, Yuri Kozyrev, told me not to worry about missing the bomb in Hilla. 'There will be plenty more,' he said by way of consolation. Many of the journalists I spoke to there seemed jaded. Now, in February, there was the occasional bombing by unidentified parties, nightly rockets at US bases around town, and the occasional IED (improvised explosive device) blowing up a Humvee on the highway. It wasn't much compared to the previous year when most of them had arrived.

Now, as everybody kept saying, it was a political story. The new constitution, the rival Iraqi leaders jockeying for position, reconstruction stories, stories about the people enjoying their new freedoms. The exciting stories, it seemed, had been done and the action had moved on. Covering the occupation was going back to being a job.

Mohammed suggested I try to get into the prison at Abu Ghraib. That was a story, he said. I spent a few days waiting at checkpoints outside different US bases in an attempt to find out who could give me the permission I needed to enter the jail. I was usually told to wait ten metres away from the checkpoint while an officer was summoned who told me that I had to go through the CPIC (Coalition Press Information Center). The staff at the CPIC would in turn tell me that they would get back to me about my request, but they never did.

Occupied Baghdad seemed a city of dead-ends and disconnections, more so than any war zone I had visited. The Western presence was largely confined to three or four hotels, the Green Zone, and the huge military bases surrounded by warnings signs in English and Arabic telling ordinary people not to approach or lethal force would be employed against them. Outside were five and a half million ordinary Iraqis, among whom were hidden a growing number of insurgents. The NGOs from the UN down had pulled out for fear of their lives. There was no one left to bridge the gap between occupiers and occupied. My jet-lag had passed long ago, but it had been replaced by a different kind of disorientation. Two different worlds co-existed in Baghdad, but they seemed to meet only in moments of explosive violence.

The inhabitants of these worlds viewed each other with a mixture of suspicion, hatred and more than a little fear.

\*

Later that week, accompanied by Steve Dupont and his writer colleague, I spoke to General Thamar, the chief of Iraqi police patrols in Baghdad. Thamar had been a policeman in Saddam Hussein's regime all his life and was frank about the new difficulties he faced, although he laughed that now the police were better paid. 'Iraqi people didn't protest before. Now we have peaceful protesting – if the same thing happened before, we would shoot them all.'

He was in command of 4355 officers who shared 615 vehicles. He said the lack of vehicles and the lack of body armour vests were his two main problems, along with a lack of radios. There was no centralised dispatch for the vehicles, so even if a crime was reported, they had no way of coordinating the cars to get there. He admitted he had never before faced a situation like the current one. He said he had not had to fire his pistol once in all the time he was a lieutenant until he became a colonel. 'Before, my guys were using AK47s, but they shot in the air.' He said their aiming was getting better now because it had to. He gave us an example. 'Last Thursday, four criminals with guns entered a house [in Al-Dora, a suburb in south Baghdad] to rape the girls. They took the gold. One family got out and called the police. There was shooting between the criminals and the police. Two killed, one wounded, one got away. All my men were safe,' he said proudly.

He said the main difference between life under Saddam and life now was that the people of Baghdad were angry, upset and often saw the new police force as their enemy. The first task of his forces today was to protect themselves. 'We have a problem, but we can control the problem. Some of my men might be killed because the police are not the military,' he said, when asked about the high rate of police deaths. It was a vague reference to the attacks by the insurgents on police. The resistance had begun to target the police force in January and February, and more than a hundred of them had been killed in the previous two weeks alone. 'These are exceptional circumstances. We have to show the people that we are here,' he said. He went on to say that when the police had first started patrolling in Baghdad two months ago, one of their major problems was being shot by Coalition troops as they had no proper uniforms and were carrying weapons on the street.

We were sitting in the garden of an old Baathist club in the centre of Baghdad. It was a Sunday afternoon, but helicopters were flying low overhead, doing circuits of the nearby Sheraton and Palestine hotels. Outside armed police guards searched all vehicles and individuals coming into the car park. The police were trying to regain control of the city. Many residents admitted that things were better since they had resumed patrolling, but to many people they were also the despised representatives of the Coalition. When we got up to leave, the general left only when two carloads of police with AK47s and machine-guns were positioned in front of and behind his car. He himself was carrying a weapon and wearing armour in the back of his four-wheel drive.

*

A few days after my arrival, I returned to the Hotel Baghdad. In the bar, one of the DynCorp cops told me that the Marines were going to go into Falluja and 'kick some ass'. I was interested in this as I was planning to go there the next day.

Walking past the dining room of the Baghdad, I was bailed up by Kurdish guards who wanted to show me something and dragged me in. On the television they were playing a grainy black-and-white videotape of a man being simultaneously beaten by two men in black – with what appeared to be metal poles – at the same time as he was being attacked by an Alsatian. The man was screaming and yelling and trying to get up, but the dog kept launching itself at him and biting him on his face and his chest and his arms. Whenever it looked as though he might make it to his feet, the two men with the poles hit him. The tape went on and on and the Kurdish guards sitting at the tables with their weapons in their hands kept pointing and saying, 'Saddam, Saddam.' It was a video looted from one of his palaces that we were watching.

Upstairs in the hotel there were guards on every floor. They had occupied a room at the end of the corridor where they had piled all the furniture and bedding against the windows facing the street, as a precaution against snipers or car bombs.

# FALLUJA

It was cold on the way to Falluja. We were travelling in an innocuous, dirty-white mid-'80s Toyota sedan, with a large crack running down the middle of its windscreen, and as we rolled down the highway at about 90 kilometres an hour, cars passed us on every side.

Dr Feisal and Salah were in the front, and I was in the back. Dr Feisal was an ex-Baathist official from Falluja. Salah, my translator, was an ex-Air Force pilot. To go to Falluja with them was costing me US$150 a day, but they knew people and I was assured that I would be safe. It wasn't the kind of place you could just drive to and start talking to people, so I had agreed to their price.

We were already running late when we got stuck behind a slow-moving American convoy. I reached for my camera as I watched a US soldier at the back of the rear truck aim a mounted machine-gun at our car. I could see his eyes – and his gun – follow my movements. I pulled my hand out of my bag without the camera. What the soldier could see was a beat-up car following him with two Iraqi men in the front and someone with a beard in the back reaching for something. As far as he was concerned, I could be reaching for a gun or even an RPG. I'd never thought how difficult that must be to watch for. I lit a cigarette with both hands in clear view and waved as we passed them.

Sheikh Rajie was waiting for us in the main street of Falluja. A well-dressed man with gold-rimmed sunglasses, he wore a tailored overcoat to ward off the freezing wind, and held a Thuraya satellite phone. It was obvious, as he waved to people in Falluja's main street and shook hands with them, that he was both prosperous and well known. His car was a sleek late-model Opel. We followed him through the town across the bridge over the Euphrates and out into the surrounding farmland. His comfortable house spread out in a U-shape, and once inside he invited us to sit in large comfortable armchairs on a spotless tile floor while a young boy wearing the floor-length shirt common in the region brought cups of sweet tea. Rajie pulled up a chair and looked expectantly at me. He began talking, as Salah translated.

'There are five important families here in Falluja and we are one of them. When Baghdad was falling, on April 9, the US asked to come in peacefully without fighting. Most of the sheikhs met the US and gave them their support. They met with them and talked peacefully. Then they [the US forces] entered Falluja ... after the agreement they had made to stay out of the town. They entered and took the school as their base ... It [the conflict] started when one of the US soldiers started looking through his binoculars. They think they are looking at the women ...' A peaceful demonstration against the presence of the US troops in the town had then turned violent when people began throwing stones at the US soldiers. The US soldiers responded with gunfire.

According to Rajie, twenty men were killed and forty wounded in the US response. According to news reports, fifteen Iraqi civilians were killed by US soldiers and fifty-three wounded between 20 April and 25 April 2003. 'Because of this accident, their families wanted to take revenge on the Americans. They started to take revenge. Each family wants to kill one man.' As the violence against the US escalated, 'the other people came in [to Falluja] ... After this accident, many people come from outside of Iraq. They come here to make operation.' The US response to the growing attacks only fuelled the hatred of them. 'They shoot everywhere with no aiming. At children. They are animals.'

Rajie claimed that most people in Falluja – a town with a population of approximately 80,000 – did not know who was behind the ongoing attacks on US forces. Yet it was clear that hatred of the US forces was widespread, and it wasn't hard to see why. In an attempt to break the networks that supported the attacks, the US had arrested all the members of the town's five most influential families. Rajie told me what had happened

when they came for his father on 16 October 2003. The
raid had begun at 2.30 in the morning in the house in
which we were now sitting, and it had involved fifty
vehicles and two helicopters. 'They started by calling out
by loudspeakers – evacuate the house or you will be
killed,' said Rajie. The members of the household com-
plied, and Rajie's father, Sheikh Barakhat, went outside
to give the waiting soldiers the keys to the house, but
they proceeded to break down the doors anyway. The
whole family was forced outside and told to lie on the
ground. Fourteen family members were arrested in
total, including Rajie, his father, four brothers and their
sons and wives. Rajie laughed when he recalled how
three Turkish merchants who had been staying in the
house at the time had also been arrested and made to
lie on the ground. All those arrested were bound with
plastic handcuffs behind their backs and rough hessian
hoods were fastened over their heads as they lay face
down in the dust. 'When they were arresting my father,
one of the soldiers put a foot on his head,' said Rajie in
disgust. It is one of the worst insults in the Arab world.

They were taken to the prison at Abu Ghraib, twenty
kilometres west of Baghdad. 'For the first five days they
put a bag on my head and chained my arms,' said Rajie,
adding that they were given very little food and water.
Except for his father, Sheikh Barakhat, who was given a
separate cell, they slept on the ground. 'After that they
took us to another place where we were not allowed to
sleep.' He explained that every half-hour a guard would

call their names and if they did not reply 'Yes sir,' they would be made to stand outside all night as punishment for falling asleep. 'There was no light, no watch. For four days they woke us every half-hour.' This treatment continued until they were questioned. Rajie was released after eleven days, as no evidence had been found that he was involved in the resistance. Today his father and four brothers were still in the prison, but he was too afraid to go and visit them and said that he wouldn't be allowed to see them even if he did go.

It was Rajie's family's connections with Saudi Arabia that most interested his American interrogators. His father had fled Iraq for Saudi Arabia in 1996 after being jailed by Saddam Hussein's regime for four years in the 1980s. His father had been one of the sheikhs who had participated in the talks to arrange the peaceful arrival of the Americans in Falluja after Baghdad fell. 'They have no evidence against us. We have relatives in Saudi Arabia. They asked if they had sent us money. They asked about the resistance operations in Falluja. They said an Iraqi wrote a report saying we have resistance connections. They asked again and again,' said Rajie.

In Rajie's opinion, the real reason they had been arrested had more to do with his father's relations with a particular American commander named Colonel King. 'He talked to the Colonel sharply and asked him to leave Iraq. My father told this man, "You told us you are not occupiers, but you have to tell us a date. We welcome you, but you have to leave." I think it is not the only reason [for our imprisonment], but the main one was my father talking sharply to this man. They accused him by [reciting back to him] his own words: "You have to leave Iraq or we will resist." Shortly afterward the family was arrested. On the same night, 16 October, two of the other prominent families were also arrested. The other two had already been imprisoned. Rajie believed the imprisonments were 'a kind of punishment for Falluja'. By the time they were preparing to rotate out of Falluja in March 2004, the soldiers of the 82nd Airborne had arrested and jailed all of the local leaders who had invited them peacefully into the town in the first place.

*

People started arriving and the servants began to serve a large lunch of many dishes. Rajie piled my plate up as everyone sat cross-legged on the floor. I was the guest of honour, and so he grabbed a handful of sheep's brains and put it on my plate. He introduced one man as the son of Sheikh Jamal, one of the local imams. The Sheikh had been arrested on the same night as Sheikh Barakhat but luckily for him the son had been out of town. Two days later he received a letter from the local civil administrator, signed by a US officer, telling him to come to the US base just outside of Falluja, one of Saddam's former properties – locals called it 'Saddam's farm'.

The Sheikh's son was afraid to go there alone and took his uncle along. The US troops let him in and he was shown his father who was briefly walked out by two

US guards and the bag on his head removed. When the Sheikh recognised his son and brother, the bag was replaced and he was taken away. His son and brother were then both 'cuffed and bagged' and taken to Abu Ghraib. The son, Hamid, was kept for fourteen days. After prompting from Rajie he described the same first four days with little food, followed by four days with no sleep, and then interrogation. He didn't really want to talk about it and occasionally between mouthfuls of food I saw him glaring at me with absolute hatred as I listened to the translator. He was thin and muscular and had a very hard look in his eyes. When I asked him what he thought of the treatment, he just replied, 'It is normal, it is a prison.' It was obvious that he didn't trust me and believed what he said would be reported back to the Americans.

While we spoke, a big heavy man with a beard and Arab head-dress kept interjecting comments. 'America rules the world, but we bring America to its knees in Falluja,' was one that I wrote down. His stream of comments made the others laugh. When I asked what the laughter was about, they told me that he was telling a story about how when he travelled to Jordan and Saudi Arabia and told people he was from Falluja, he didn't have to pay for taxis or hotels. People offered him free meals. Their resistance to the Americans was a badge of pride.

Rajie excused himself after lunch and I sat smoking with an older man from another of Falluja's oldest families. Khalil Mohammed worked on the local government council; he was in charge of the town electricity supply. He had been elected to the position by the people in his area; it was a voluntary position for which he received no payment from the Americans. 'The problem in Falluja and elsewhere is that the Americans do not explain themselves to the Iraqi people. The US people have the idea that they are the masters of the war. If I want something from them, I have to keep silent and agree with everything. It is very difficult to deal with the American mind.' He explained that in Falluja there was a lot of pressure on people to be publicly against the Americans. 'The people want to work. They want medical services. They want schools. If they have these things, the killing will stop. Most of the people in Falluja, if you ask them openly, will say that they are against the Americans,' he said, waving to the others we had just finished lunch with. 'But if you ask them privately, they do not want to go back to Saddam times. They are afraid to announce their real ideas. A lot of people [involved in the insurgency in Falluja] come from outside Iraq. He [the average person in Falluja] is afraid for his family, for himself, his reputation ...'

He told me the story of one old man, Hesham Aluwzi, who was killed in early February. He had gone to the Americans on the behalf of others, 'to the US base asking about the people in the prison. He was dealing with the army and went frequently to the base. They killed him because he helped the Americans.' As for himself, Khalil said he wouldn't go anywhere near the Americans. One day, in June 2003, the US Army came and cordoned off his area. They searched his house and his shop among many others, breaking the lock of the shop. When he returned, a journalist from the *New York Times* was there asking questions, and the people there told him to say that the soldiers had stolen money, which he did. He wasn't proud of what he had done, he said, he was just afraid of these other Iraqis whom he didn't know.

Rajie interrupted us. He wanted to talk about his father, who was still in jail. 'This is the idea. They have to make an example of Sheikh Barakhat because he is very famous here. He is the big leader. Mr Bremer said we will start a new page with the Sunni. But even the criminals have more rights.' He said there had been no contact with the sheikhs from Falluja inside the prison and that he and others were trying to organise some kind of delegation to go to the Governing Council to find out what had happened to them. 'The Americans just follow their desires ... the other sheikhs, important sheikhs, they take them and then nothing.'

*

The office of the Governor of Falluja was across the road from the bullet-scarred and barricaded police station. As Salah and I waited for Rajie and Feisal to arrive in the other car, gunshots rang out, very close and evenly spaced somewhere along the winding, almost deserted street. The guards at the gate of the governor's office didn't even look up as the shots rang out. 'There is no security here,' said Salah flatly as we waited on the exposed street. The shots could be anything, he explained – someone cleaning their weapon, shooting a dog or perhaps an argument of some kind. There was nothing to stop anyone doing what they liked here. The police were holed up in their walled police station still recovering from the recent attack, and the US troops were at their base about five kilometres out of town to the east. On the street there was just the occasional car and the two guards who let us in to the bare building that served as the governor's office.

We were ushered into a side room and told to wait. Bored-looking men – most of them armed – sat around the cold office drinking tea. They were the guards for the few people still working in the office. I asked if we could see the governor, but nobody was sure if he was there. The previous governor, Raid Alibraza, had been arrested by the Americans three days after the attack on the police station on 14 February. The governor had submitted his resignation the day before the police station attack and to the Americans that meant he had been involved. They hadn't liked him very much in any case. According to the local chief of the justice department in Falluja, Machmud Ibrahim Hassan – who happened also to be waiting to see the new governor – Alibraza was a tough guy with the Americans: 'He always stuck to his word. Sometimes they agreed with him. Sometimes he gave orders without informing the Americans. Most of the orders were dealt with the security situation, some with arrested people. He resisted the Americans arresting women. They didn't like that. They took him to Baghdad.'

An aide to the new governor now came in and told all of those waiting that the governor was in Baghdad and would be until further notice. They, and we, stood up and prepared to leave. It was no surprise. The new governor ran the risk of being attacked in Falluja and he had rarely been seen in the office since his appointment. Government had stalled, and the new governor was afraid either of being killed by his constituents if he appeared too pro-American or of being arrested by the Americans like his predecessor if he tried to speak up for the people. It was a no-win situation for the governor who, the others joked, was in Baghdad collecting his money.

*

Spending a night in Falluja was not an appealing prospect, so we drove back to Baghdad. Early in the morning we headed straight back to the main street of the town to meet Sheikh Rajie for breakfast, at what he insisted was the 'best kebab shop in all of Iraq'. As we ate our way through mountains of grilled tomatoes, barbecued meat and salad wrapped in flat bread, Rajie held forth on the problems afflicting his town. There were no foreign contractors and no aid projects running in

Falluja; the violence had started before any of them were established. He waved at the main street outside the window: 'Look, there are no women here on the street. It is too dangerous for them.'

Another man joined us in the busy restaurant while Salah translated. He pointed to a shop a few doors down and told us that in November a US soldier had been shot on the sidewalk by a shopkeeper with an AK47. 'The other soldiers were shocked and did nothing. Before they could open fire, the shopkeeper got away,' said the man, who wouldn't give his name.

As we sat at the window, Rajie pointed out a building where the US had tried to establish a base in the town but had been forced out. As he talked, two Humvees sped past. Even though we were right across the road from the barricaded police station, several men in the restaurant jumped to their feet and ran outside. The next thing we heard was crackling gunfire from the street. The sound followed the Humvees as they sped through town, but it was ineffective and the vehicles kept going.

'Don't worry, they will attack them at the crossroads. They always do,' said Rajie, still eating the kebabs. He was referring to an intersection near his house, where a Blackhawk helicopter was shot down on 8 January 2004, killing all nine on board. The Americans now called it the 'death triangle'.

Things had been relatively quiet in Falluja since the attack on the police station, but the roads outside the town were another story. Mortar attacks and shooting occurred every day. The violence was perpetrated by both Iraqis and Americans. A seventeen-year-old boy introduced by Rajie told me one such story. In early February, on the road to the town of Habbaniya, he had approached a US checkpoint. The American soldier manning it 'waved his hand for us to pass and then after three or four hundred metres he started shooting. The same man – he started shooting,' the boy said, adding that three people were injured in the four cars passing through the checkpoint, but even though bullets hit the car he was travelling in, he was not hurt. Rajie commented dismissively, 'When you pass a convoy and pass the trucks, the first one in the convoy almost always shoots. There are tens of these incidents every month.' No one really kept a count, least of all the US troops.

We kept eating and drinking tea and finally left, all of us piling into Rajie's car. We were going out of town to the Jordanian Hospital, almost opposite the American base. Rajie insisted we travel in his vehicle because it was well known. Trucks and towtrucks were lined up on the outskirts of the town. 'There is no work here,' said Rajie, waving towards them. 'To work with the Americans means you will be attacked. There are two steel factories in this area. No work now. The cement factory is only working a few hours a day now. No contracts.' We pulled up at the walls to the Jordanian Hospital and waited in line with the other vehicles. The walls were scarred with gouges from the big .50 calibre shells from an American machine-gun. US soldiers had opened fire from the nearby base when they saw some cars full of armed men chasing someone down the highway in December. Unfortunately it was the Iraqi police in pursuit of someone who had just attacked the governor's office in Falluja. Between eight and ten police were killed by the misdirected US fire, as was one Jordanian soldier standing guard at the hospital.

The Jordanian officials at the hospital didn't want to talk about that incident. In fact, they didn't want to talk to the press at all. I was trying to get some idea of the level of violence in Falluja, but the officials wouldn't speak until the director arrived. When he did, he politely told us – over yet another cup of tea in the small demountable that he was using for an office – that he could only give us the total figures of patients they had treated. He told me that they saw on average between 1100 and 1500 patients a day and had performed 800 operations since they arrived in April 2003. More serious cases were evacuated to Baghdad or Jordan. He wouldn't tell me how many people were treated for gunshot wounds. 'You must understand, everything is political here. I will have to check if I can tell you that,' was all he would say. He made vague reference to sending me the information, which he never did. It is likely that he was afraid the figures would reveal the extent of the casualties, which would offend the Americans.

The Jordanians at the hospital, like everyone else in Falluja, were in a difficult position. They often treated victims of the conflict, and they were at pains to stress

that they never asked what had happened when someone was brought to them. The Americans pressured them
to hand over resistance fighters, but if they did this it
would make the hospital itself a resistance target. It said
a lot for the respect the local people had for the Jordanian operation that the only time it had come under attack
until then was from the US forces themselves.

At the town's other hospital, in Falluja itself, there
were no guards, just a line of battered old white ambu-
lances. We walked straight in through the open doors
and were shown to the director's office. Dr Abdul Jabar
al-Hadthy was the second in charge and had been working there for fifteen years. He spoke perfect English and
immediately ordered tea for us. Since the trouble had
started last April, 175 people had been brought to the
hospital and died as a direct result of gunshot or explosive wounds. He didn't keep records of how many
people were treated and lived, he said, but on the day
of the attack on the police station he treated thirty-four
people with severe gunshot wounds.

On an average day they admitted anything between
two, three or as many as ten people with gunshot
wounds or multiple wounds from explosives. 'The hospital itself is very old. It was built in 1963 and develop-
ment has been limited. The main problem is the lack of
support from the Ministry of Health. We have shortages
in human resources – specialists. We have no specialist
plastic surgeon, neurologist, chest and heart specialists.
There are lots of burns victims and those injured in

the war. The crew of the surgery just deal with it however they can, but they are mostly general surgeons and orthopedic and ear, nose and throat specialists.' He went on to list a range of shortages of equipment, from simple surgical instruments to the external frames needed to set limbs shattered by explosions and gunfire, to the fact that their donated X-ray machines were broken.

They had received the machines from an NGO shortly after the Americans had arrived, but because of the security situation nobody returned to fix them when they broke down. Dr al-Hadthy said that the Americans from the local garrison had helped them with some basic supplies, but this had not amounted to very much. 'The only real solution is to build a new hospital,' he said. There were only seventy-three beds in the hospital and with the current levels of violence they needed at least 400. The doctor did agree that it had been relatively quiet lately. I didn't have the heart to tell him about the planned Marine operation I had heard about in Baghdad, but he probably knew about it already.

*

In the centre of Falluja the graffiti on the walls read, 'Long live our leader, all Iraq belongs to Saddam' and 'There is no God but God and America is the enemy of God'. In the old part of the town the alleys were so narrow that you could barely drive a car down them, let alone a Humvee. I was taken to the shop of a man called Ali Achmed, who sold fertiliser. We drank tea and he echoed what many people in Falluja said. 'America created this problem. It is their idea. The Americans created the resistance by arresting these people.' He said that when the Americans arrived, there was no freedom, only more killing. 'They promise to help the city with electricity, to give jobs, but there is nothing.'

He complained that the fertiliser factory had closed, that his produce was six times the price it once was, that 50 per cent of all the workers in Falluja had once been involved in agriculture and now there were no jobs. 'Yes, we are proud of the resistance,' he said. 'America makes some promises – democracy. Now we only have the weak and poor Governing Council. Garner said we will have a new government, and then one week later they kick him out. Then Bremer, new strategy. The resistance is a kind of punishment for the broken promises of the Americans. All the Iraqis support it.'

In Falluja, people were afraid of the Americans, he said. Even now, talking to me, how did he know that the Americans would not come and catch him for what he had just said? 'For all Iraqis, the major problems are security, education, health. There is nothing on the horizon to solve these problems … When the Americans came, there were some who said "The fire of Saddam is better than the paradise of occupation," but others have just been treated badly so they have joined the resistance. The resistance is not to bring Saddam back. Those who were against Saddam are now also against the Americans.'

We left him in his deserted shop with no customers and barely any fertiliser to sell and drove slowly out through the maze of streets where the only traffic was the occasional donkey. This was supposed to be the worst part of Falluja where the US forces never came. It was just a poor ramshackle neighbourhood of one- and two-storey flat-roofed buildings with streets too small to get through in an armoured vehicle. That was why the area had been left alone.

\*

In the centre of town Humvees had moved into position around the police station and there was a detachment of US soldiers on the roof with guns pointed in all directions. Salah, Feisal and I parked the car next to the pile of barbed wire that blocked the side street. Feisal in his tweed sports jacket and Salah clutching his small leather filofax tried to look as dignified as possible approaching the Iraqi police guards, who were very young and very nervous. The stretch of ground outside the police station felt like a shooting gallery for the jumpy police and there was absolutely no one around except the guards and us. One, wearing a bandana around his head, kept saying 'Boom Boom' over and over again and laughing. The way they held their weapons casually by the straps and waved them around and started yelling at each other in confusion when we asked to see someone was very disconcerting. Eventually an officer arrived and told us to leave. The

American commander was in a meeting and no one would be allowed in to see him.

The Iraqis had claimed that when the police station was attacked, they asked the Americans to come and help them. The Americans claimed they had received no calls for assistance. Whatever the truth of the matter, the fact was the American base was only a few kilometres down the road. At the very least they would have heard the gunfire. The town they were supposed to be guarding was suddenly occupied by a determined force of several hundred men blocking off streets and attacking the police station to release the prisoners and it still took them three hours to come in to town. Understandably the police felt as though they had been left in the lurch. The US forces refused to comment at the time.

I tried another entrance while Salah and Feisal decided to stay in the car. The US soldiers wouldn't let me in and, in fact, wouldn't even let me come within ten metres of them. I stood in the empty street and tried to tell them that I was a journalist, all the while thinking that one of the guys from the kebab shop was probably going to shoot me for trying to make contact with the Americans. For their part, the soldiers on the roof were already aiming at me. When I thought I could at least take a photo, they told me to move my hands away from my bag when I reached for my camera. As usual they told me to contact their Public Affairs officer. But he of course had already rotated out.

The US military in Falluja really didn't want to talk to a journalist, at least not to an Australian one. My subsequent attempts to meet with or even to contact them produced nothing but a few emails that informed me the Public Affairs officer for the 82nd Airborne had left the country. They referred me back to Baghdad, where I was told again to contact the Public Affairs officer. Of course, due to secrecy, the Marines Public Affairs officer couldn't admit to me that the Marines were being sent to Falluja, and besides they couldn't talk to you unless you were embedded. They weren't at that stage taking any embedded reporters, and if they were, they would have to be for American outlets only. In time I gave up on the idea of trying to cover both sides of the Falluja story.

One of the first casualties of the Marines' later operation in Falluja was a local journalist, Burhan Mohammad Mazhour (working for the American ABC network), who was shot neatly through the centre of his forehead by Marines as he tried to cover their first attempts to move back into the town.

# SIGNS OF TORTURE

Rajie's story of his treatment in Abu Ghraib – and all of the other accounts – had a sickeningly familiar ring. For the last three years I had been covering the Indonesian military's attempts to put down separatist movements in Aceh and West Papua. I had heard many stories of people disappearing into detention without any charges, trials, release dates, visits, or any sort of accountability on the part of the jailers. In Indonesia I would usually try to find a human rights organisation or a legal aid worker who could help to verify the accounts of those who claimed to have been victims of the military. In Iraq in early 2004, it wasn't so easy.

The United Nations had left Iraq after the devastating bombing of their Baghdad headquarters on 19 August 2003. Twenty-two people had been killed, including the head of the mission, Sergio Vieira de Mello. Similarly the Red Cross had left after their office was bombed on 27 October 2003, killing forty people. This had precipitated a flood of departures of most of the NGOs working in the country. The only authority that remained which had access to Abu Ghraib and the other detention centres was the Coalition Provisional Authority itself. Associated Press had reported on 24 February 2004 a statement by Army spokesman Colonel William Darley that seventeen US soldiers, including a Battalion Commander and a Company Commander, had been suspended from duty pending the outcome of an investigation into the abuse of prisoners. Aside from that, little more information was available. Those who questioned Coalition spokespeople regarding the nature of the charges were politely but firmly brushed off. In late February I found that even obtaining a reliable figure of numbers of detainees was difficult. I was given alternate figures of 8000, 10,000 and 12,000 by three different Coalition spokespeople.

Only one organisation, called Occupation Watch, seemed to be trying to work on human rights issues and still had staff in Baghdad. I organised to meet Paola Gasparoli, their spokesperson, at the Al-Fanar. No one, it seemed, had offices anymore or rather they didn't tell people where they were. They didn't want to be blown up by car bombs. As soon as I met Gasparoli, she launched into what she was working on. There were, she said, very serious abuses taking place throughout the detention system. Often the treatment for those picked up was worse if they were detained in the base of the unit that had arrested them. There was one place that was particularly bad about which she had a lot of information. It was the base at a former refinery in Dhora, a suburb of southwest Baghdad.

There, she said, detainees were not entered on the detention logging system. No record existed of their detainment. They were mostly people picked up in sweeps by the troops based in the area. 'They line them up against the wall and then shoot between them,' she said, as an example of what she'd heard. She went on to outline one account from the Dhora refinery that she regarded as very credible. It came from a man who had been working for a London television producer as an assistant. His wife had contacted Occupation Watch in an attempt to locate him after he had been arrested. In the first week of January 2004, the man had been taken to the base with his son after being caught in a 'cordon-and-search' operation in the Baghdad suburb of Hadimiya. In such operations troops would block off entire areas with armoured vehicles and arrest all those in the designated buildings. The pair were taken to the refinery and told to line up in the open and stand to attention. 'They tell the son and the father not to turn their heads and to repeat the rules,' said Gasparoli, who added that the son forgot to repeat the rules properly and was immediately beaten to the ground and kicked in the testicles.

The same father and son were then taken to an old Scania truck factory near Dhora, now also a US base, where the father was told by the US troops that he was not going to be put with the Iraqis being tortured.

He saw Iraqis squatting in groups as they were given electric shocks by US soldiers with cattle prods. Every time the men went to sleep they were kicked, and every time they were moved they were dragged. It was a program of continuous humiliation for the first day or more. The prisoners were kept in the open and given one MRE (US military Meals Ready To Eat) per day.

The father and son were eventually released with eleven others out onto the highway at 11 p.m. with their IDs confiscated and their money not returned. There was no official record of their ever having been detained.

The accounts of prisoners kept coming back to sleep deprivation and the use of bags over the heads and handcuffing as the standard procedure for anyone who was detained, regardless of what for. Gasparoli had accounts of thirteen- and sixteen year olds being detained in this way. T-shirts were tied around their heads and tightened if they complained, and water and food simply stuffed up their noses.

'The whole problem', Gasparoli said, 'is that this term "security detainees" does not exist in international law.' The treatment involved no obvious breach of international law because of the way the US had relabelled its detainees as security threats rather than as prisoners-of-war or even criminals. 'There is a sense of impunity in the behaviour of the US troops. Even though they put these seventeen on trial, it hasn't made any difference to the stories I am hearing of this treatment every day.'

Paola Gasparoli didn't necessarily go hunting around for stories of maltreatment of prisoners. They were something that continually came to the fore in her work. In fact she was attempting to monitor the compensation system that was being set up by the CPA to try to deal with the huge number of claims against the Coalition forces for damages and loss of life as a result of the occupation. The claims system was being run through the offices of Civilian Military Operations Centers, otherwise known as CMOC. The offices were staffed by Iraqis working for the CPA who were supposed to be the first point of contact for those seeking redress. Many of those who went to the offices sought information on detained family members. Helping these people had become part of the role of the centres. They were also places where people could be found who had stories to tell about mistreatment. It seemed that anyone going to the centres had a bad experience of the Coalition forces.

Unfortunately for Gasparoli, she had been banned from the CMOC centre near the Dhora refinery. The staff informed her that she was a 'radical human rights activist who was not acting on behalf of the Iraqi people'. They had no doubt been encouraged by their superiors to take that line. At the time the direct superior of those running this particular office was an Iraqi woman who worked in turn under the direct supervision of Brigadier Janis Karpinski, the commanding officer of the Abu Ghraib prison.

After talking to Gasparoli, Salah and I drove around central Baghdad for the rest of the day. She had told me about a group called Christians for Peace, apparently a group of American fundamentalist Christians who held regular protests on a roundabout in central Baghdad. They were protesting the inhumanity of the US occupation and had taken up the cause of the detainees. I was told I would find many former detainees to interview if I could find the protest. But we never did, and instead spent most of that afternoon in central Baghdad stuck in traffic.

I was getting to like Salah. He always had an interesting anecdote or story to tell whenever we were marooned in our car, which seemed to be most of the time when we were out trying to work. On this particular day we were in the shopping district of Al Karrada, not very far from the downtown area where the major hotels are located. Al-Karrada is a shopping district and anything from washing machines to wide-screen TVs, computers and satellite phones are available. Since the war in 2003 there had been no taxes on imports and the prices for consumer goods were well below international norms. As we waited, I noted a pile of small electric ovens on the pavement. Salah recalled that not so long ago American soldiers would come here, walk around, do some shopping, eat pizza in the restaurants and buy things such as refrigerators for their bases. 'But then one day, about two months ago, they were walking around talking, buying things like bicycles, toys for their children, and three young men came from that street there,' he said, pointing. 'They attacked the US vehicles and then ran into one of the buildings. The Americans burned down the building, all three storeys.' Sure enough, as the car inched forward in the traffic, we moved slowly to the front of the burnt-out three-storey building. The American soldiers don't go out shopping anymore in Al-Karrada, and you rarely see a foreigner on the street except for the Yemenis, Egyptians and Sudanese who still come to Baghdad to trade and make money.

# KARBALA

The tenth day of Muharram was approaching. The Shiite festival of Muharram involves forty days of mourning for the death of the founder of the Shiite religion, Hussein, killed in battle in the Iraqi city of Karbala in the seventh century. The tenth day – the day on which he was killed – is the defining day of the mourning cycle. It is marked by the gathering of Shiite pilgrims in the holy city which, along with the city of Najaf, is seen as the birthplace of the Shiite religion.

During the time of Saddam Hussein, the ceremonies of Shiite mourning – pilgrims flagellating themselves with metal chains while praying, and then beating themselves with ceremonial swords as the mourning reaches a fever pitch on the tenth day – were banned in Iraq. After the regime fell in 2003, the practices were revived and the ceremonies were reinstituted in Karbala and Baghdad, with thousands of Iranian pilgrims crossing over into Iraq to attend them. In 2004 the festival of

Muharram promised to be even bigger than in the previous year.

The mourning ceremonies had begun a few days earlier in Baghdad. I wandered around the Khazimiya Shrine in Khadamiya, watching the pilgrims with their wooden-handled flails to which chains were attached. With each step taken in time with the beating of the ceremonial drums, each man took another swing of the chain around his shoulder. One shoulder at a time, synchronised with everyone in the line, so that at each step the chains rose and fell in unison with varying degrees of force against each man's back according to his degree of religious fervour. Some men slammed the chain so hard into their back that you could see their whole body stiffen at the blow. Others seemed merely to swing it over their shoulder as if swatting flies.

US troops were stationed at the entrance to the area around the shrine. They were behaving in a low-key and respectful manner, keeping their distance. When I entered the area, my bag was searched and I was patted down for weapons by young men wearing badges from the mosque denoting their status as security. It was all relatively peaceful. For the first time since I had come to Baghdad I felt comfortable walking around unaccompanied. At the entrance to the shrine – beside a young man selling popcorn – was a large portrait of Mohammed Bakr al-Sadr, a hero to the Shiite people who had been killed by Saddam Hussein in 1979 after being arrested in 1976. His nephew was the cleric

Moqutada al-Sadr, who now commanded a wide following among Shiites, based in part on the legacies of his uncle and his father, Muhammed Sadiq al-Sadr, who was assassinated in 1999.

I left Khadimiya when it got too dark to take photos and walked out past the tour buses full of Iranian pilgrims. It had been a very orderly and serene ceremony.

\*

1 March 2004: We left for Karbala with the sunrise and sped down the near-deserted back highway. I was travelling with another journalist, Stephan Faris, from *Time* magazine. We passed the occasional destroyed tank or anti-aircraft gun, left where they lay after their destruction by US forces on their northward advance to Baghdad in March and early April 2003. It took us barely an hour to cover the hundred or so kilometres to the outskirts of Karbala. We drove fast, because the road was notorious for thieves. As we waited at the first checkpoint, while armed men in civilian clothes searched vehicles, our driver joked that we could keep going on this road all the way to Saudi Arabia. He had spent time working there and wanted to go back. He said he would be happy to keep going and leave Iraq behind him forever.

We started to see groups of people walking along the side of the road. Big tents had been set up with large cauldrons over fires in front of them – way-stations for the pilgrims, where they could eat and drink tea before resuming their walk to Karbala where they would celebrate Ashoura, the mourning of the death of Hussein.

It was expected that this year there would be attacks upon the pilgrims. The targets of bombings had been shifting more and more from the Coalition itself towards those Iraqis who sided with the Coalition or were employed by the new government it was trying to put in place. Police stations and individual officers, recruiting centres for the new Iraqi military, government buildings, people on their way to work for the CPA, contractors and Iraqis working for those engaged in the reconstruction projects – the list of potential targets had widened considerably in the six months since the bombings had started in earnest. Now it was speculated that because of the perceived support for the Coalition's efforts by the majority Shiites, they would be targeted. So strong was the expectation of violence that the pre-eminent Shiite leader, Grand Ayatollah al-Sistani, had issued a *fatwa* or religious order banning Shiites from attending the ceremonies. But the order was widely ignored, and as we arrived thousands of pilgrims already thronged the narrow lanes of Karbala's old city.

My hotel in the old town overlooked the gold domes of the main shrines where most of the pilgrims would congregate. After checking in, Stephan and I headed out again to see the local Iraqi police. The streets I walked through were blocked to traffic and there were lines of men, mostly unarmed, who had been organised by the mosque to provide security. They were supposed to search everyone who came in and out of the closed area of the old city that contained the two holy shrines and the narrow streets that ran in a circle around them, but often they just waved people through. They were identifiable only by small badges on their clothes. At the edge of the old city were guards armed with AK47s who halted and diverted traffic away from the blocked streets.

At the nearest police post we introduced ourselves to the local police commanders, Major Heidar Ismail and Captain Abdul Amir Najar. They escorted us into a bare sitting room with a few chairs and an old couch. The captain did most of the talking. 'We have a security procedure and we don't expect any violence,' he said. 'We expect the terrorists to attack us every day – not just during the celebrations.' Even so, today was a special day and they were ready. He said that although they hadn't arrested any 'terrorists' yet, the borders of Iraq were open; the police believed some were already here or about to arrive. We asked which countries they were expecting the terrorists to come from and received the usual answer: 'From all countries around Iraq because there is no security at the border.'

The idea of searching the growing crowds for terrorists or people carrying weapons seemed to irritate him. 'We don't want to annoy anybody by attacking them with searches. We look for suspicious behaviour.' He said millions of people were in Karbala that day and the responsibility to search for terrorists didn't rest with him; there was a special police department for terrorism. 'We cannot be aggressive. We have to be humanitarian. Karbala is so sensitive because there are so many Iranians. We are only here for emergency response in a big situation,' he said. He noted that Polish, Bulgarian and American troops were based outside of the city due to the religious sensitivities of the people, and that the job of the police was to 'block the area ... We've got emergency doctors.' The police had clearly handed over responsibility for the security of the area around the two shrines to the Shiite groups.

*

The crowd was now thick throughout the old city and the densest mass was near the shrines where large groups of men had started to chant and thrash themselves. The crowd was so thick here that I had to push my way through those watching the chanting. I headed for the small office in a portable trailer in between the two shrines.

The office was in a small gated area, and the gate was blocked by a stern-faced man with an AK47. Others stood behind him with radios, dressed in quasi-military attire. A crowd was pushing against the gate and the guard was having trouble holding them back. Behind us was some kind of commotion. As we waited, the crowd parted for two men who roughly pushed another man through the gate. He had a black beard and was dressed in the black robes of a Shiite cleric and was arguing in

Farsi with his two minders as they pushed him. We watched while one of the two who had brought him waved a black Makarov pistol. It appeared that the two men had found the man in possession of a gun at one of the checkpoints. He was an Iranian cleric and very angry at the way he was being treated.

Stephan and I and our translator were allowed to slide in through the people pressed up against the gate arguing with the guards. Inside we were led to the trailer and told to wait outside. The guards were armed and a few had radios, but there was a lot of arguing going on and it took some time to find out who was in charge. Eventually we were invited in to speak with the man in charge, who sat cross-legged on the floor of one of the rooms with his aides beside him taking notes. He was dressed in the robes of a cleric and introduced himself as Seyd Jawal Naji, the head of the Security Council for the two shrines. 'We find the thieves before the police find them because their destination is the shrine. Thieves, heroin, criminals, all the types of criminals. We open our eyes today for everything. Yesterday we arrested a murderer, a thief who killed somebody for money.'

We asked him about the possibility of attacks. 'For sure the terrorists will come, but we are ready for anything. We have to be careful. We expect them. They will come, our intelligence says. Karbala will be so crowded that we are sure they will come tonight.' He said that 'about four or five [were] arrested today and yesterday. Two days ago we arrested a car bomber at the end of this street outside the shrines. He said he was working for Saddam and he supported al-Qaeda.' He said this man would be handed over to the Americans. Two other terrorists had also been arrested, one with a car bomb two months ago and the other at the Coalition base outside Karbala one month ago. He admitted that there could be a problem, but said they had been preparing for this day for the four months that he had been in charge. 'You can say this day is the most important. Yes, we will be a target tomorrow or today. We hope Hussein will protect us and we will do our best to protect ourselves.' Our interview was over and we were moved quickly outside.

In the enclosed area near the office the arrested cleric sat glaring and the guards tried to hold back the crush of people now trying to get in through the gate with complaints and enquiries. It took us a few minutes to push our way out through the dense wall of bodies.

*

The crowds of people were flagellating themselves to the beat of the drums. The black-clad pilgrims, the onlookers weeping for the death of Hussein, the crush of people in the streets around the two shrines – as the afternoon wore on, it became so crowded that it was impossible to move in a direction other than the one in which the crowd was moving, which was normally in a circular motion around the shrines as its members struggled to be allowed in to pray. In the side streets of the old city, away from the crush around the shrines, people were everywhere, sitting on the ground or sleeping in doorways or the verandahs of shops. Crowds of men stood drinking tea, and food was being cooked in massive cauldrons over open fires in the streets. All were planning to spend the whole night praying, chanting and singing. At some stage the select brave devout men would replace their wooden-handled flails with swords and begin to rhythmically beat their foreheads until blood ran.

After dark the crowd was so dense that it took Stephan and I over an hour to negotiate the distance of several hundred metres between our hotel and the shrine security office. We returned there to find a small patrol of four men; but the gate to the security compound was so crammed that we couldn't get near it. A patrol leader, Sergeant Khidier Toma, told me that they had recently received information about a bomb in a red car – a Caprice to be exact. 'They cannot drive it inside. Hopefully we can control everything,' he said. He said the police had arrested three more people and found three car bombs, one in the morning and two in the afternoon. 'We have patrols everywhere,' he said.

I was starting to have my doubts about the information we were receiving. It sounded like so many rumours; no one could actually say what was going on or what had happened. The police were saying it was the job of shrine security and the shrine security were relying on the police. Literally thousands upon thousands of people were crushed into the streets around the shrines.

It was impossible to move your arms above your head in the worst parts, as they were pinned to your body by the weight of surrounding bodies. There was no way this place could be patrolled or secured.

We moved around the streets near the mosque. It took a lot of pushing, through crowds that were becoming more frenzied in their devotions to the dead Hussein. Women watching the men were now weeping openly; all were wearing black shawls. Some people who identified themselves as members of the Bader Brigade, an Iranian based Shiite militia, told us that four days ago they had discovered a police car with a bomb at a checkpoint. They said they had arrested two men from Zarqawi's group, the Jordan-based affiliate of the al-Qaeda network that the Americans routinely blamed for every bombing. It was impossible to check any of this but the rumours intensified the feeling of impending violence. Now the Bader people were saying they could not trust the police.

At the same time followers of Moqutada al-Sadr, the radical Shiite cleric, were chanting anti-American slogans. My companion, Stephan, and I stopped two of them and began asking questions. They replied, 'We want an Islamic government. We are not looking for a government like Iran's. We don't want the constitution to be Islamic.' They started to spell out the main grievances of Moqutada al-Sadr. 'The Governing Council doesn't represent the Iraqi people. The Governing Council are all appointed by the US. They didn't suffer like we did here ... We want a government elected by the Iraqi people. The Iraqi people will vote for an Iraqi president, Sunni or Kurd. That's okay, we don't want to separate them.' Stefan, an American who had introduced himself as an Italian, began asking questions. He was exasperated by the simplistic answers he received. 'What do you want the US to do then?' he asked. 'We want them to leave today. We don't accept the occupation. Its only justification is that they say there will be chaos when they remove Saddam. But Iraqi people are proud there is no sectarian violence.' Then they returned to the more familiar daily complaints of the Iraqi people. 'One year since the occupation! Still no electricity. Still no security. We will reject any law from the Governing Council. The law should come from a group that is elected.'

The two men, both poor Shiites in their mid-thirties, were representative of the disenfranchised followers of al-Sadr. They had been repressed under Saddam and now they perceived that they were being excluded from the political process being put in place by the Americans. Stephan had spent much time in Najaf profiling some of the Shiite leaders. He said that the attitude of the two al-Sadr supporters mirrored the standard line of their leadership. The US was to blame, there should be immediate elections, the Governing Council was illegitimate. Interviewing them made him frustrated. He felt their attitude was blinkered and did not take into consideration that the Americans were trying to help the country and wanted to leave as soon as possible. They threw his questions back at him: 'All the millions of people you see here are protected by Iraqis, not Americans. The US causes chaos at the borders, they don't want elections, they don't provide services.' We shook their hands and moved on and forced our way slowly through the crowds back to the hotel.

*

The chanting, drums and singing kept me awake. I tried to sleep but got up at about two in the morning and went outside. The city was still crowded with people. Some had fallen asleep in small groups on the pavement. Others were grouped around the tea stands. Some were still chanting, flagellating and marching. Women were still crying for Hussein. I thought I heard gunshots as I wandered around the back alleys. I had no translator with me so I wandered alone through the crowds who were all in their own advanced stage of religious fervour and exhaustion. It felt good to be out at night, and I began to enjoy the carnival-like atmosphere. People chatted quietly down the side streets, drinking tea and eating sweet cakes. They were all waiting for the early hours of the morning when the beating with swords would begin. Most of the people, including the thousands of Iranians, had nowhere to sleep – no intention of sleeping, in fact – and the streets were still crowded when I returned to the hotel after four.

At breakfast the photographers were grey with exhaustion. There were flecks of blood on their clothes.

They had been up all night to get pictures of the flagellations. On the roof of the hotel I watched the pilgrims come staggering out of the shrine. They had been marching around it for hours, since before dawn, slamming the flat of the ceremonial swords into their foreheads in homage to the dead Hussein. Some had gone further in their devotion and used the sharp side; I could see deep gashes in their heads and blood flowing freely. The ones who did this were dressed in white and marched in the centre of the road. They had by that time been going for hours and their white clothes were covered in blood that ran through their hair and down their faces and backs.

From up on the roof we watched them as they emerged from the final shrine. Although they were supposed to stop beating themselves at this point, some kept going and going. They would be grabbed by men who had been assigned to remove their swords and stop them injuring themselves further. They were staggering by this stage and blinded by the blood and the blows to the head. You could see some collapsing, and an ambulance coming and going, forcing its way through the packed street to collect the latest who had fallen.

In the street it was the same crush but people were now nearly delirious with exhaustion. I went with a translator to the main temple. Outside, the crush of people was so intense that I felt the crowd carrying me in through the entrance and my feet being lifted off the ground. I lost Maithan, the translator, in the crowd and had to brace myself against the wall of the temple to stop being forced in. I heard the first explosions as, gasping for air, I made it through the other side of the wall of people, back into the less crowded street.

*

The first two explosions were distant and brought barely any reaction from the crowd around me. A few people looked up, but most kept praying and chanting or struggling with the crowd to get into the shrine. I walked quickly back to the hotel along the edge of the crowd. In the foyer of the hotel the guests were still sitting and chatting, but the guards looked nervous. I took the lift straight to the roof, and just as I walked out onto the flat rooftop a third bomb went off and I heard screams and saw a cloud of black smoke two streets away. I ran straight back to the lift. In the lobby screaming people were forcing their way in through the door and the room was crowded with people looking shocked and afraid. I saw two of the photographers forcing their way through the crowd at the front door onto the street and I went after them.

As soon as I reached the street, a wave of people running away from the explosion crushed up against me. I saw the open glass door of the hotel behind me smash as people pushed against each other to get in. The guard tried helplessly to stop them. My legs were knocked out from underneath me and it felt as if I was pushing against a furious undertow in the sea. I kept moving to the pillar that held up the verandah of the hotel. It was like a breakwater from the panicked crowd that flowed around either side of it. Then, just as I looked up, a bomb went off not more than 100 metres away. The bright orange flash was in the middle of a street still densely packed with black-clad pilgrims who had been fleeing one blast only to be caught in another.

I reached the bomb scene not more than a minute after the explosion. The flood of people escaping the first blast had swept past. The only ones left were those who had been caught in the explosion, and they were lying on the ground injured. I'd felt the heat from the explosion on my face. The panicked crowd had run the other way and suddenly the road was clear, so I simply walked over to where the bomb had gone off. Pieces of bodies lay all around the intersection. In the middle of the road one man sat upright, even though his body seemed to have split down the side like a ripped seam. Blood poured from his sides and his head onto the road. He was still alive but dying in front of me. It was suddenly quiet and there was no one near, just that man along with bodies and parts of bodies and another man lying on the ground with his legs kicking in a reflex action who – I think – was already dead. I saw what was a severed small child's hand, half-shredded and wet, lying on the blood-covered road. There was no sign of the rest of the body. I was shaking and trying to hold my camera still. Under my foot I felt something slippery and my heel skidded. When I looked down, what I saw was unmistakable. It was part of a human brain.

I gagged and my eyes filled with water as I tried to steady the camera and not throw up.

I took some photos and tried to count the bodies. I counted seven but there were so many different parts that I couldn't be sure of anything. I was standing there shocked when an angry man ran up and started to shout at me in broken English: 'This was no car. Believe me, the Americans drop this bomb right here. I see this.' The man who had been upright and dying fell over and people started to approach slowly. Some who were carrying shrouds placed these over bodies. To one side a fruit stall was burning furiously and a man was waving us away. Then another loud blast came from a few streets away. I ran to the other side of the intersection and a man pulled me over and said, 'There were six bombs. They moved them in here by handcart.' His name was Raad al-Khalidy, and I wrote the name down shakily, taking up almost a whole page.

I kept walking around the corner to the other bomb-site, the one I had seen from the roof. It wasn't far, just on the next corner. I saw a leg with a shoe. Blood that had been sprayed up the front of a shop was now dripping back down. A drop landed on my notebook, and I recoiled and immediately wiped it off. Underneath the same awning that was covered in blood were the large bags belonging to the pilgrims. Two people with headscarves covering their faces were already trying to rip open the bags to steal their contents, although there were still parts of bodies lying in front of them. I moved away, both scared of them and already beginning to hear more explosions further out in the city. The last ones sounded like mortars. As I walked down the centre of the street, three rolling crashes came from somewhere out near the police station. I tried desperately not to step on anything that had once been human, but this was difficult as there were parts of bodies everywhere.

\*

Further down the street, towards the shrine, people were starting to lay shrouds and cloths over the bodies. I counted nine but couldn't be sure if the cloths covered whole bodies or just parts of them. There were still more uncovered corpses on the ground. A police utility drove up the street with men with Kalashnikovs on the back firing into the air. From the shrine I heard more gunfire and saw people running. Now out of film I turned back towards the hotel, but a cordon had been put in place around the most recent bombsite, blocking my way. As I tried to pass, screaming guards waving guns high above their heads surged through the people and grabbed the camera around my neck. Holding the camera with one hand, a guard tried to bring his gun butt down on my head with the other. I started yelling 'Sahafi' (journalist in Arabic) and grabbed the camera strap to hang onto the camera and stop him choking me with it. More guards came running, screaming at me. When I replied in English, the crowd around me grew thicker and I could feel punches on my back and pushing from all around.

The crowd was yelling 'Mossad ... CIA' and pushing against me. The guard kept trying to hit my head as I deflected his gun butt with my free hand. The camera strap was pulled up over my head and I let it go and the guard fell back. I tried to grab it and he went to hit me and I jumped back, falling into the crowd. He waved me away, screaming abuse, and the crowd watched as I retreated.

As I came out of the crowd closer to the hotel, I saw some of the *Time* photographers. They just stared when I told them what had happened, and then went back into the hotel. The translators said they couldn't help and everybody looked shocked and scared as the screaming on the street outside grew louder and more frenzied. Somebody came into the hotel saying the crowd had killed a foreigner. For all we knew it was an exaggerated account of the assault on me.

The atmosphere on the street was now crazed. Several Iranian pilgrims were being beaten and their cameras confiscated by the shrine guards who were trying to cordon off the blast site right outside the hotel. The guards were just as shocked and as scared as everybody else was. At least two other foreign news photographers were also assaulted in the area, I found out later.

*

The attack had been timed to hit at the exact moment when the exhausted crowds would be finishing their all-night ceremony after they had worked themselves into a state of physical and mental exhaustion. The reaction to the bombing was charged with an insane fear and panic. In the chaos, the Shiite authorities reacted by blaming anyone in the area with a camera or anyone whose presence there they could not understand. But there was also an immediate blaming of the Americans and a certainty that they were behind this horrible attack on the people. It was terrifying to be on the receiving end of this. I am certain that if I had continued to struggle with the guards over the camera they would have beaten me to the ground and the crowd would have joined in. They wanted a focus for their outrage. There was the shock, too, of their ceremony being destroyed by bombs exploded in an area where the only thing that could absorb the blast was people themselves, trapped in streets too crowded to flee from. It was horrible.

We went up to the roof of the hotel, as there was little else to do. The drivers and the translators told us to stay inside. They were not from Karbala and all but two of them were not Shiites, so they too felt under threat. I wanted to go out and try to get my camera back from the guards, thinking that they might have calmed down and that the film might still be intact. Yuri Kozyrev from *Time* said simply, 'Don't go now, it is not a good time.' He lent me his Thuraya satellite phone so that I could file a report. When I called the paper in Australia, the people there had already heard about the bombings on the wire services. There had also been bombings at precisely the same time at the Khazamiya Shrine in Baghdad, and the editor, close to deadline in Australia – though it was barely 11 a.m. in Iraq – wanted to know exactly what I could tell him that he didn't already know. I gave him a quick rundown, then hung up, sat down with a cup of tea and wrote an account in my notepad. Then I called back the copytaker and dictated it to her as I sat on the roof.

From up there I could see the crowd on the street re-forming outside the shrine. The guards were still shouting and grabbing people, and there was the occasional shot fired into the air by a guard telling the crowd to get back. Shock had turned to anger and then to a kind of sullen defiance. The crowd was aggressive and some of its members were yelling or chanting slogans. I remember one translator telling me to get away from the side of the building lest I be shot. Stephan went out to try to find out what had happened. As he went, he cheerfully told me that there would be no problems as he was 'Italian', not American. His translator looked worried. I grabbed a lift back to Baghdad with Yuri and his driver Mohammed, who drove his eight-cylinder Chevrolet station wagon at breakneck speed, leaning on the horn to get the other slower cars out of the way. There were checkpoints outside Karbala searching cars, but they waved us through and beyond them were Polish armoured cars on the highway.

Everyone was quiet in the car as we sped out of town; there was an unspoken anxiety about the drive ahead.

I was thoroughly spooked and couldn't wait to get out of Karbala. I had never been so relieved to drive in a car with such a big engine. The following day local radio reported that twenty kilometres outside of Baghdad eleven civilians in a minibus travelling on the same highway from Karbala had been killed by unknown gunmen.

In Baghdad that night I went out on the balcony to smoke a cigarette and finally worked up the courage to take off my boots. In the worn-out heel of one of the boots there was a small cavity where stones often got stuck. I just knew something horrible was stuck in there. When I looked, I could see it was a piece of brain or flesh from the street in Karbala. I flicked it out with my pen and began to gag. I stood up, leaving my boots, and went inside to bed.

# AFTERMATH

2 March 2004 – the day of what became known as the
Ashoura bombings – was at that time the worst day of
violence since the premature declaration of the end of
hostilities by President Bush on 1 May 2003. Over 200
people were killed and 500 wounded in attacks in
Karbala and Khazamiya in Baghdad. That night CNN
played loop footage of US troops being forced back by
crowds of angry Shiites in Baghdad immediately following the bombing. The media pundits of the West
were in Baghdad for the signing of the new Iraqi constitution, and there was no shortage of print and television references to the possibility that the bombings
would start a civil war.

On the day after the bombings I returned to the
Khazamiya Shrine with Salah. Hundreds of black-clad
Shiites had gathered in the streets around the shrine. As
we walked towards it, we were stopped every thirty
metres or so by rows of armed civilian security guards

and patted down for weapons. Absolutely everyone on the street was stopped – it was like shutting the gate after the horse had bolted. The previous day's bombings were the only topic of discussion. One guard began to tell me what had happened: 'I was there inside. I was a guard at the gate yesterday. I saw a woman praying, and then I saw the same woman with her head cut off. For two minutes I couldn't do anything. Then I was very confused. I couldn't pick up the bodies. Arms, legs and heads. I couldn't count the number. One of them was a pregnant woman whose baby get out from her.' He was starting to sob as he spoke, but he kept going: 'As you know, more than fifty people were killed. That all happened inside. Who is the terrorist? What is the benefit of this death of Iraqis? It is very much blood. I am wondering, somebody say it is America, al-Qaeda, Saddam. Nothing is clear.' He gave his name as Ibrahim Ali, a thirty-three-year-old resident of the surrounding suburb. He was crying by the time he had finished, a tough man clutching an AK47 and openly weeping as he remembered the things he had seen after a suicide bomber had entered the shrine and blown himself up in the middle of a crowd of worshippers. The people in the street looked sympathetically at him and his colleagues. The other guards simply patted him lightly on the shoulder.

Crowds were moving along the streets in groups, chanting Shiite prayers and slogans to Hussein. Long diatribes were coming from loudspeakers up and down the street outside the shrine. It was a show of defiance.

We had to talk our way through another three lines of makeshift security to enter the small winding alleys beside the shrine walls that led to the house of the imam. Outside his house we were told to wait, and the guards filled in more of what had taken place. According to them, there had been some shooting between unknown civilians and the Iraqi police on the outer cordon around the area at around 5.30 a.m. In the confusion, as the guards responded and the crowd panicked, the bombers slipped through the cordon and put themselves in place around the shrine. There were four or five bombs, including one that was placed very close to the imam's residence that they had managed to find before it exploded.

In all the confusion of the initial shooting the police left their positions and the crowd attacked their cars. One man was seen throwing grenades from an abandoned hotel. He was caught by police and then – the guards added conspiratorially – shot dead by a stranger. The police retreated to the outer cordon, and foot patrols by the police or the US soldiers stationed at the end of the street were stopped. The only security after that were the helicopters flying continually overhead.

Then, at around ten o'clock – exactly the same time as the detonation of the Karbala bombs – the explosions started in Khazimiya. The major explosion was inside the shrine itself and that was the one that had caused the most deaths. Another two were set off by suicide bombers in the immediate vicinity of the shrine. A fourth bomber, apparently a Syrian, was captured by the guards as he tried to detonate himself. The aftermath was similar to that in Karbala: pilgrims and worshippers, many of whom had been up all night, became frenzied.

In Khazimiya, however, a target for their anger appeared almost immediately, as American Humvees tried to approach the mosque from the outside cordon at the end of the street roughly 700 metres away. According to the guards, the US soldiers came down towards the shrine, shooting in the air. 'The crowd was very angry. They were not afraid of the US soldiers.' The soldiers were pelted with rocks and bottles until they retreated outside the cordon and back into their base across the road. According to the guards, at least three Iraqis were killed by gunfire from the Americans. Foreign reporters in the area were chased out and roughed up by the aggrieved crowd.

\*

At the end of the road the American soldiers were still standing behind the barricades outside their base that they had pulled back to on the day. To my surprise they were friendly and polite when we walked up to the gate, allowing Salah and myself inside immediately. 'You guys okay? You need some water or something. We had an AP [Associated Press] guy running in here yesterday when everything was going on,' said the sergeant in charge. They gave us water and sent for a Humvee to take us to speak to the commander.

They were a newly deployed unit from the 2nd Brigade, 1st Cavalry Division, and they treated the area outside the barricades as a hostile zone. The commanding officer, a Hawaiian, Lieutenant Colonel Myles Miyamasu, came down to meet me in the briefing room.

Miyamasu was a short, lively man and seemed very willing to talk. He launched straight into a description of the previous day's events. 'After 0700 we had our men stationed at the first traffic circle here out the front. We were approximately one block from the shrine. That was our last presence, we didn't have anyone in there. Then we heard the explosions and ICDC [Iraqi troops] they were manning the gates, and some Iraqis stopped by and told them what had happened.' He was eager to set things straight. 'We saw it on CNN. That was how we knew what had happened. We had no intel in there, and we organised to send some medical support teams. We went down there to provide medical support between 10 and 11 a.m., and obviously the people did not want us out there so we pulled back. Earlier the ICDC had fired warning shots at the crowd.' I asked him about the guards' claim that Iraqis had been killed by US fire. 'Our forces did shoot to break up the crowd and the possibility of ricochets was there,' he conceded. 'As I said, we ran down there with our medical assets and it was a very hostile situation. When we started to establish our medical post, we packed our gear and the crowd turned. They were throwing rocks, chairs, anything they could get their hands on.' He added that they had also heard

AK47 fire coming from the crowd. 'You know, I've watched that footage of Israel and the stones being thrown at Israeli troops, and yesterday when that happened I was thinking of that. I was thinking this is what it is like,' he said. 'You had several thousand people upset, you had rhetoric going from loudspeakers saying Coalition forces caused the explosions.'

After the troops pulled back to the base under a hail of objects – which was filmed by CNN from a nearby rooftop – people continued to try to attack the troops at the gate of the base. 'We had about 2000 people pushing up against us. One individual charged us with a pickaxe. They stoned us. They threw two Molotov cocktails. It went for about two hours from start to finish,' he said, giving credit to the Iraqi police and the Iraqi troops for calming the situation. He said it had been a mistake to try to go in there with medical aid. 'Look, I think in regard to what happened yesterday, I would not consider going in to give medical assistance unless there are thousands wounded,' he said after I asked if he would do the same thing again.

It was a microcosm of how the US forces, acting with good intentions, were succeeding in little more than making the situation across the country more volatile. Ordinary Iraqis, with their fragile pride and their unfocused outrage, interpreted the offer of assistance as an insult. The US forces, secure in their bases, would now be more reluctant to offer assistance in the future. I thought that the lieutenant colonel was honestly trying to give his side of the previous day's events. Outside the Iraqi guards at the shrine were saying that the US troops had been pushed back. The local people were saying that the number of Iraqis who had supposedly been killed by the American troops as they defended their withdrawal back to their base was anywhere between three and fifteen, depending on whom you spoke to. The footage of his men being pelted with stones and reversing their Humvees up the street was still being replayed on CNN as a visual for analysts talking about the failure of the US efforts in Iraq. The commander had seen himself as being in a place where a large number of people nearby needed medical assistance and he was in a position to provide it and that was what he had tried to do. He hadn't thought his men could become a target for the confused and angry crowd. It had never entered his mind. As he said, 'We were getting all our information from CNN.'

The lieutenant colonel was called away and we chatted with a captain who stayed with us. He told us that four or five times a day the base was hit either by mortar rounds or by RPGs. But it was a large area, so they rarely did any damage. Most of the mortars came from the direction of the Sunni area called Adhamiya, and occasionally the brigade would go out and conduct cordon-and-search operations there. On that day they were busy. There were five reported IEDs (improvised explosive devices) that they had been called in to check out and disarm, and they were in the process of dealing with one at the main telephone exchange. That particular bomb later exploded, causing local phone networks to go down for a day or two.

When we walked out through the main gate of the base, the first thing we encountered was a loudspeaker across the road. Followers of Moqutada al-Sadr had set up a tent draped with black prayer flags and were reading out statements to a small crowd. 'Down with the Coalition, we want to cleanse them,' was the loose translation Salah gave me when I asked what they were broadcasting over the loudspeakers. It was the al-Sadr supporters' crude form of psychological warfare, designed to stop people approaching the base. Salah wasn't paying enough attention to translate properly for me because – unbeknownst to me – people were threatening us as we walked past. They had watched us come out of the base and shake hands with the US soldiers and now they were saying we were spies. Salah stopped me from pausing to buy cigarettes and we walked away hurriedly to our car.

\*

The US administrator, Ambassador Paul Bremer, wasted no time in making a statement about the bombings. On the evening of the day of the attacks, he said that, 'The terrorists have murdered and maimed on one of the holiest days of the year.' They had done this to provoke sectarian violence, and they had chosen this particular day in order to kill as many innocents as possible.

Why would they do this, he asked, and proceeded to answer his own question: 'The terrorists want sectarian violence because they believe that is the only way they can stop Iraq's march toward the democracy that the terrorists fear.'

He slipped back into familiar territory: 'We know that the terrorists fear democracy because they said so. In a recent letter the terrorist Abu Musab al-Zarqawi wrote that democracy was coming to Iraq and that once Iraq was democratic there would be no pretext for attacks. And so Zarqawi has admitted that the terrorists are in a race against time. It is a race they will lose. They will lose because the Iraqi people want and will have democracy, freedom and a sovereign Iraqi government.'

Since it had been made public in a CPA press conference on 10 February, Zarqawi's letter had been the pillar of the Coalition's attempts to blame the violence on foreign, al-Qaeda-linked terrorists. Throughout February 2004, at almost every press briefing, the Zarqawi letter had been brought forth as evidence that the problems Iraq was facing were not rooted in the Iraqi people's rejection of the US-backed Governing Council. Instead they were the work of foreign terrorists determined to cause the Iraqi experiment in US-enforced democracy to fail. Yet, as one *New York Times* journalist remarked after yet another briefing, 'How do we know the US didn't write the Zarqawi letter themselves?' We didn't, we simply had their word for it.

Now, after the Ashoura bombings, Bremer was again using the threat of al-Qaeda terrorism to reinforce US policy in Iraq and to suggest that they were fighting the same enemy responsible for September 11 and international terrorism. It was a dangerous self-delusion, leaving the Americans on the ground in Iraq with an easy way to explain the rising tide of violence without ever having to question their own part in it.

According to Bremer, we were winning. We just had to hang in there, the Iraqis and the US together, and things would soon be fine.

\*

'An Iraqi government is coming. This week, after an appropriate period of mourning, the Iraqi Governing Council will sign the Transitional Administrative Law. That law brings with it all that the evil-doers fear: They fear an Iraqi government controlled only by Iraqis. They fear equality before the law for all of Iraq's citizens. They fear democracy. After the law is signed, Iraq's journey to a future of hope will continue. On June 30, the Coalition will turn sovereignty over to the Iraqi people. Next year there will be three elections and Iraq will end 2005 with an elected government sovereign throughout the Land Between Two Rivers.'

Representatives from the Iraqi Governing Council were making a statement on the previous day's bombing. The statement followed the standard daily briefing from Brigadier General Mark Kimmitt and the representative of the Coalition Provisional Authority, Dan Senor. Attending the briefings was always a drawn-out affair, as you had to enter the Green Zone. I always felt bad leaving my translator, Salah, outside the entrance gate for an unspecified period of time while I vanished inside. I could never say with any accuracy how long I would be, as it was often a lengthy process just getting through the gate. Bomb scares were frequent. No matter how far the Coalition forces extended the security zone, or how many concrete blast barriers and dirt-filled blast bags they set up around the entrance, there was always going to be a point where ordinary Iraqis would have to be allowed to approach. At that point there was the possibility of a suicide bomb attack.

As it was supposed to be the government of Iraq, they couldn't exclude all Iraqis, which would have made the security job much easier, so instead the CPA guards made everyone without special permission or an escort wait in a long queue in a kind of corridor created by blast bags. The first checkpoint was manned by Iraqis, with a US soldier in attendance to check for weapons. Then came the open corridor of blast bags with a gun trained down it at those waiting. If there was a delay, people got nervous here, as a concealed bomb could be ignited and those waiting could still be fired on from the street. Often there *was* a delay. At the next post Americans checked IDs; visitors were frisked and bags emptied and checked. In deference to Muslim culture, a woman was always on hand to pat down the women going through.

Another ID check followed as you walked into the Green Zone, and then there was a final ID and body search before entry was allowed to the Conference Center where the briefings were held. Needless to say, the process could take anywhere from ten minutes to an hour and a half, and once in you thought twice about leaving.

The Conference Center was a large, modern, three-storey building with escalators, lifts, meeting rooms and auditoriums. It had been purpose-built by Saddam and was, like most of the buildings in the Green Zone, a former government building. The Green Zone itself was ten kilometres square. The roads were empty except for Coalition military traffic and the odd CPA civilian four-wheel drive. It was the only part of Baghdad in which officials could drive safely, and virtually no Iraqi civilians were to be found there.

Although some Iraqi civilians still lived inside the Green Zone or came in every day to trade at a small market or work for the CPA, none of them were stupid enough to walk around the long, wide streets that connected one former government compound with the next. I entered by the wrong gate one day and found myself questioned constantly by passing military or CPA officials as I walked down empty streets overgrown with weeds. It seemed the only way the Coalition could create a safe environment in which to govern Iraq was to remove all the Iraqis.

Brigadier General Kimmitt commenced the 3 March briefing by discussing yesterday's bombings. Kimmitt, the deputy director of operations for the US military in Iraq, had the lean look of a lifelong soldier. His clipped delivery and straight-talking demeanour belied the shrewd mind of a professionally trained spin doctor who could turn any question, no matter how contrary to his message, into an opportunity to re-state the Coalition's goals or achievements. Although his jerky formal movements made him resemble an unthinking automaton, he was actually very accomplished, a perfect spokesman for this mission.

There were more journalists than usual and more rows of cameras on tripods in the well-appointed auditorium. Long rows of benches were equipped with microphones for questions, and small wireless boxes with headphones for translations were available to whoever wanted them. Kimmitt finished his rundown of the attacks by declaring, 'We will kill or capture those responsible.' This was an oft-used phrase. He was asked why the security had failed to prevent the bombings. 'All persons involved in security believed they had made sufficient preparations,' he replied, adding that he had close to 200,000 Iraqis and 100,000 US troops working to ensure security. Asked if he thought the handover of sovereignty could go ahead given the obvious security problems, he responded, 'The political process will continue. The more we empower the Iraqi people, the harder it is for the terrorists to gain ground.' It was the standard line of the administration. 'The plan to hand over sovereign government, the plan to hand over sovereignty, is on track,' he said. He answered a question about who was responsible for the bombings by talking about Zarqawi. 'We have evidence specifically linking Zarqawi. We are working on this. We have solid evidence linking him to twenty-five previous attacks.'

Kimmitt said that the FBI was being called in to assist the investigation. When asked again if Zarqawi was responsible for the previous day's attacks, he conceded that, 'We never directly attributed these actions to al-Qaeda.' It was the kind of muddy reasoning he always offered. If asked about bombings, he spoke of Zarqawi and al-Qaeda, but the truth was no one had been charged and they really didn't know who was behind them. How could they? If Coalition forces had tried to go anywhere near the bombsites in Karbala or Khazimiya to investigate, they would have been set upon by an angry mob. Whether they called in the FBI or not, they still didn't know who was responsible.

Finally Kimmitt tired of the questioning about the security and who was responsible for allowing the attacks to take place and said, 'If you wanted absolute security, you could have achieved that by cancelling the festivities. Had we cancelled these festivities, the terrorists would have won.'

Next was the Governing Council briefing. The Shiite member of the Governing Council spoke first. He said that Colin Powell had called him to pass on the condolences of President Bush. He spoke of the horrible injuries he had witnessed at Karbala the day before and

he spoke of the legacy of al-Hussein himself and how
those killed had been attracted to Hussein in the struggle against oppression and the revolution of human
rights. He compared Hussein to Gandhi. 'Al-Hussein
stands with the martyrs. We stand with our feelings
now. We never thought we would see real martyrs. They
have gone to heaven. Now they think Shiite will accuse
Sunni. There is no Sunni who stands in this. We are not
afraid of these plots, these conspiracies.' He spoke from
the heart, I thought. He was trying to combat the spectre
of communal violence between Shiite and Sunni that
everybody feared was taking hold of the country. He was
also trying to claim the dead in Karbala and Khazimiya
as martyrs for the cause of a new democratic Iraq – the
country the Americans were trying to create through the
Governing Council.

Ahmed Chalabi was next. Chalabi, who had admitted
to being paid by both the Pentagon and the CIA; who
had supplied false information on the existence of
WMDs to the Coalition to justify the war in the first
place; who, as almost every Iraqi would tell you, was
considered little more than a crook in his own country.
Chalabi came across as a competent professional politi-
cian, eloquent, witty and now appropriately grave. He
began by saying that when the bombs exploded, people
feared that Saddam had returned and that he was
slaughtering people. 'We have so many hands and feet
we don't know to whom they belong,' he said, empha-
sising the chaos of the bombings. Then he reverted to

his standard line: 'What's happened is an evolution in the fight against terrorism ... the only way to defeat those who do this is to hurry up the democratic process.'

He was building up to the same point Bremer and Kimmitt had hammered home: 'Let's not forget the letter of Zarqawi published in the media.' He said that it was impossible in Iraq to create civil war of the kind that the likes of Zarqawi wanted. 'Those who want to play on the chords of sectarianism will fail,' he declared. 'We are nowhere near civil war and we will never have civil war.' His message was one of acceptance of the Americans and their program. 'If we talk about security in this country, whether we like it or not the security has to be in the hands of the Coalition.'

The briefing wound up and thankfully Salah was still waiting outside. We drove to the Al-Hamra Hotel, getting caught in traffic along the banks of the Tigris, while Salah pointed out the buildings that had once been nightclubs. He told me that he had seen Demis Roussos perform in one of them. Sometimes he would get lost in his reminiscences of the old days before the Iran–Iraq war began in 1980. He was a young man then, a pilot in the air force. There were casinos and night-clubs in Baghdad. Back then he had even been a drinker of alcohol.

There was more to this, however, than rose-coloured recollection of youthful times. He was trying to explain and to show me that things hadn't always been like this. There was a time when international stars would come and perform. You could tell, looking around Baghdad, that the period of the late '70s was the last time when there had been anything like the normal life that we know in the West. Restaurants, hotels, houses – all the décor seemed to be from that time. It was before Iraq was plunged into the conflict with Iran, an event which was, for males of Salah's generation, as devastating as World War I was for Europeans. The figures of the dead from the eight-year war have been conservatively put at 105,000 Iraqi and 262,000 Iranian troops. In a country of less than 20 million, the Iraqi army grew during the war to 1,250,000. All men of military age were conscripted. During this time, too, Saddam's internal secret police grew in size; many joined it voluntarily to escape front-line duty in a conflict characterised by bloody trench warfare, gas attacks and high casualties. When the war finally ended with a ceasefire in 1988, only two years elapsed before Saddam invaded Kuwait and the Gulf War followed and nothing was ever the same for Iraqis again. Sanctions, the occasional bombing and increased repression by Saddam were fixtures of daily life in Baghdad until the 2003 war and the American liberation. Men like Salah, who was in his forties now, had to cast back twenty years to recall a time when Baghdad was 'normal' – when they had nightclubs and they were not fighting a war or under international isolation.

Needless to say, in early 2004 there were no nightclubs along the banks of the Tigris. The Green Zone was on the other side of the river, and if a nightclub had

opened and not been destroyed by a car bomb or a
suicide bomber, chances were it would have been hit by
return fire from jumpy US troops across the river. The
closest thing to a nightclub now was the coffee shop that
overlooked the pool at the Al-Hamra Hotel, the other
hotel besides the Sheraton and Palestine frequented by
journalists and contractors. Among the latter were those
employed by the CPA to rebuild the infrastructure and
those employed to protect them – a lot more of the latter,
usually. 'Contractor' in this case was merely a polite way
to refer to a mercenary, a hired gun.

Although it didn't have the ostentatious security of
the Palestine, there were always many South African,
Australian, British and American gunmen hanging
around out the front to protect their charges. I'd told
Salah I was trying to meet someone, but I really just
wanted to sit somewhere quiet for a few minutes and
have something to eat and drink. I was still rattled from
the day before and I suppose it showed, because an
Italian photographer I had met in Karbala asked me if
I was okay and looked at me with a kind of quizzical
concern. He told me that some other photographers had
also been roughed up, and that a guy from the Gamma
agency had taken the best pictures of the day. It made
me feel worse for having lost my camera and film. I
ordered some food and waited with my beer, then at
8.05 precisely two very loud explosions rattled the windows in the restaurant. They were mortar rounds going
into the Green Zone across the river. I never found out

more about them as the Coalition, as usual, made no comment. Such incidents happened almost every night and, if asked, Coalition spokespeople would almost invariably reply that they were unaware of any 'uncontrolled blast and no Coalition casualties have been reported'. Later that night as I lay in bed I heard small-arms fire and the distinctive heavy return fire of US .50 calibre machine-guns. It seemed that Baghdad, after the worst day of violence since the Americans arrived, was getting back to normal.

# DEMOCRACY IN THE MAKING

On Friday, 5 March 2004, the Transitional Administrative Law – which outlined Iraq's new interim constitution – was due to be signed at a special ceremony in the Conference Center at four in the afternoon. An Iraqi choir would be present, as would all members of the Governing Council and the senior members of the Coalition Provisional Authority. Reporters were supposed to be there two hours before the signing and were to be locked in until the ceremony was completed. Security was very tight in all of Baghdad, with roads blocked and a greater than usual number of vehicle searches holding up traffic. Helicopters swooped so low over the roads that you weren't aware of their presence until they came over your car and then the sound hit your ears. By then the helicopter was already way past, and you could see it through the front windscreen. Salah and I were running late after an unsuccessful trip to the interior minister. After waiting for a long time and finally being allowed into the ministry compound in Baghdad's southwest, we were informed that the minister was not in the country, for his own security. It came as a surprise, because we had seen him two days before when we had made a tentative appointment, but Baghdad was like that. It was very hard to arrange anything.

Driving back into the centre of town we were once again stuck in traffic in the middle of a shopping district. Being Friday, the Muslim holy day, few shops were open but plenty of people were milling around. Suddenly, on the curb only four feet from our stationary car, a man broke away from two Iraqi policeman he had been talking to and started running. The police, instead of giving chase, aimed their AK47s at the man and fired one shot after another directly at him as he ran off through the crowd. The crowd didn't dive for cover or run. They just watched, with only a few ducking and moving away slightly to the side out of the trajectory of the bullets. The man got away and the police didn't give chase. Salah shrugged and lit another Viceroy cigarette and began telling me a story about his sister who had once lived in this area. She was robbed, and then the robbers had returned to sell her goods back to her. When she refused to pay them for what had so recently been her property, they threatened her with a gun. She ended up moving, he said, ending the story with his usual comment: 'There is no security here now.'

We were late, and although it was still more than an hour to the signing of the constitution, the US soldier on the gate wouldn't let me through. After I called him some unflattering names, he summoned his superior who was about six and a half feet tall with a flat, large face covered in fresh scabs as though he had just fallen on a rough patch of bitumen. I was annoyed and told him the only reason I was a few minutes late was because his army couldn't secure the city and the traffic was terrible and that he should let me through. He told me in no uncertain terms to leave the gate immediately. He was in no mood for exceptions. They were on high alert and apparently there had been a security scare while getting the Iraqi choir in through the gates.

I was locked out of the Green Zone. I decided to go instead to see the imam from the shrine in Khazimiya. Imam Ali was in and happy to receive us. The same guards we had spoken to on the day after the bombing led us through to a cramped office. We removed our shoes and took the proffered places on the floor. The imam began by saying that the explosions and the frenzied reaction against the American troops were part of the same plan: 'They tried to start a fight with the Americans.' He himself had not met with the American commander despite what the commander had told me. The imam said that as a follower of al-Sistani he didn't think it was appropriate to meet the US forces. 'There is an occupation now. When that is over and the new government is established, but for now we refuse,' he said.

The imam blamed the attacks solely on the Americans and began to make comparisons. 'The Taliban and

Bin Laden were created by the Americans as a reason
to invade Afghanistan. Then there is the timing of the
bombing in Baghdad, Karbala and in Pakistan. Bin
Laden, Zarqawi, Saddam supporters – there is a connection between them. Who pushes them? Maybe Mossad.
I don't know. There is no stability in Iraq for a long, long
time,' he said. He was saying the conditions that created
the bombing were in some sense the work of the
Americans.

But there was a positive aspect to this experience, he
said. 'These kind of bombs and incidents give the Iraqi
people the power to secure their own areas – as you see
coming in here, with all the young men. We employ
simple methods of searching. Under the Muslim rules it
is forbidden to kill. Those who bomb on the tenth of
Muharram are not Muslims at all.' He said that while the
people were angry and upset over the bombing, they
were happy if they were killed in this way at the shrine.
'Saddam's people stopped this ceremony in Najaf and
Karbala and here for thirty-five years – even the injured
people say that when they recover they will get back and
they will not be afraid of the bombing and what will
happen. Gandhi, he is not a Muslim, but he learns from
[the seventh-century holy man] al-Hussein to get victory,
to win the battle. He is following Hussein's example to
get the victory, even though they wanted to kill him.
When we get into one of these shrines, we are starting
with Adam or Moses or Jesus or Mohammed. We are a
peaceful people. We don't want to kill anybody.' He was

preaching forgiveness, not just to me but to those in the room, the guards and his staff. 'The people on the tenth, when they hit themselves with the chains and the knives it is a holy act. It is meaning no injury to anyone ... Mohammed said Hussein is from me and I'm from Hussein. The people who join Hussein, some of them are Jews, some are Christian. Hussein was asking for peace and to get together with all the nations to advise the people to keep them away from violence.' For the moment his message of tolerance was working in the Shiite community of Khadimiya. But for how long would moderate calls for peace on the one hand, and blaming the Americans on the other, even by the moderate clerics who supported Sistani, be able to hold people back from attacking the Americans? The explosion of violence against the American troops in Khadimiya following the bombing might well have been encouraged by those who wanted to disrupt the American-controlled political process, but the fact was that everybody had joined in very quickly and nobody had tried to stop it. The most likely result of the imam's policy was a growing frustration among the Shiites that would drive them towards groups such as Moqutada al-Sadr's which advocated fighting the American occupiers.

We spoke for a long time until he excused himself for the afternoon prayers. He asked me what my religion was and then told me that the bombing of the shrines was the equivalent of suicide bombers entering the Vatican. How would I feel as a Catholic if the Americans occupied Rome and failed to provide security, he asked. 'Of course you would blame them. It is normal.' As we got up to leave, he asked my nationality again and responded, 'Australia. It is so sad you are still under the British. We defeated them many years ago.' It was a joke. He was referring to the 1920 Shiite-led uprising, which had taken place when Iraq was a British protectorate.

The Shiites in Iraq comprise more than 60 per cent of the population. Under Saddam they were marginalised and kept out of powerful positions in government and subjected to harsh repression. When they rose up against Saddam after the 1991 Gulf War, they were cruelly repressed after the US failed to support them after initially indicating that it would. Bitterness towards and suspicion of the US remained strong, and that afternoon it was four Shiite representatives of the Governing Council who refused to sign the Transitional Law. At the last minute they objected to the inclusion of clauses that guaranteed the right of the Kurds to have their own language and which did not address the issue of Islamic law. Many commentators felt they were just flexing their muscle and showing Bremer and the CPA that they could, if they chose, derail the process leading up to the 30 June handover of power. Inside the Conference Center journalists were locked in and unable to leave as officials tried to negotiate for the signing to go ahead. CNN was reduced to showing live pictures of the empty table on which the document was supposed to have been signed.

*

The Iraqi Governing Council announced that the signing would now go ahead on Monday, 8 March. Pressure was being brought to bear on those who were not signing, and manoeuvring began between the different Shiite groups both inside and outside the council. Chalabi apparently made a visit to al-Sistani in Najaf to try to get his representatives to sign, but nobody knew yet whether the signing would take place. It was all a grave embarrassment to Bremer, who had made many statements about what a landmark the Transitional Law was on the path to Iraqi self-government. Over the weekend the CPA fell silent concerning the prospect of the interim constitution being passed.

That Sunday night, at the *Time* house in the suburbs of Baghdad, I saw on the newswires that large explosions had been seen near the Conference Center in the Green Zone. I immediately hitched a ride there with photographer Yuri Kozyrev and his driver, Mohammed.

The explosions were already on the wires because the fireball could be seen from across the river at the Palestine Hotel, where most of the journalists stayed. Ten rockets had been fired at the Al-Rashid Hotel, near the Conference Center and just inside the Green Zone. It had been a place where senior officials of the CPA had once stayed, but after a rocket attack in October narrowly missed US Deputy Secretary of Defense Paul Wolfowitz and killed a US colonel and injured fifteen others, it had been deemed too dangerous and was now empty. The problem was, the Al-Rashid was too close to the outer perimeter of the zone and could be hit from any one of the residential apartment blocks across the road. But the US could not return fire on the apartment blocks – right across the road from the Green Zone was too public a place for action of this kind.

When we arrived, US troops were blocking the road and diverting the traffic. We pulled over, and I got out to ask what had happened. A US soldier was waving traffic off to a side route and another walked up to another small Japanese sedan that had stopped but not turned and was trying to inch its way forward past the soldiers. 'What the fuck do you think you are doing, motherfucker?' screamed the US soldier. He had stuck his body into the front driver's window and was screaming in the faces of the occupants. He was a big guy and his bulk was increased by the body armour so that he could barely get himself inside the vehicle. But he did it and he was slamming on the roof with his free hand and waving his gun in the other and swearing like hell at the occupants who probably didn't speak English. I asked the other soldier what had happened. 'We don't know anything, sir. We were just told to stop the traffic flow.' Behind him there was a vehicle burning on the street and Humvees and soldiers gathered around. Back in the car, Mohammed sped off in another direction to go to the other side of the checkpoint.

At the entrance to the Conference Center, we found a US officer talking to some journalists. Behind him the street was blocked by armoured vehicles. As the cameras gathered, Lieutenant Colonel Randy Lane spoke: 'I think there are definitely people who are trying to stop a new Iraq from emerging,' he said. He explained that eight to ten rockets had been launched from a vehicle on the street and had hit the Al-Rashid Hotel. The rockets had been fired from the back of a truck that had either exploded of its own accord or been destroyed by gunfire from the perimeter of the Green Zone, he wouldn't say which. No one knew if any Iraqis had been killed.

The journalists had raced down here because it was the night before the signing and the explosions made a good news piece to tie in with it. It was also a location, right outside the Conference Center, that everybody knew. 'I imagine some people are trying to break apart what the Iraqi people are trying to achieve,' said Randy to the cameras. He looked good in his helmet and vest with his weapon and the armoured vehicles behind him, and I saw him on television for the next day or two.

Every time the Coalition tried to announce a milestone or an achievement, something like this happened, and it was to the insurgents' credit that they knew exactly how to get the media to cover it. Then again, the people who hit the Al-Rashid knew where the journalists stayed and they knew the signing was happening the following day, so it wouldn't have been too hard to organise a stunt of this kind.

There was no point hanging around any longer and we headed off. But by now the surrounding streets were swarming with ICDC troops forming roadblock after roadblock. They ordered us to stop and told us to get out of the vehicle. We tried to explain that we were journalists, but it made no difference. Mohammed our driver tried to explain too, but he was shouted down in a language he didn't understand. The soldiers were Kurdish, and here they were in the middle of Baghdad aggressively ordering people to stop and roughly searching them and their vehicles. To Mohammed it was an outrage. They were treating him as a suspect in his own city.

Large numbers of Kurds had enlisted in the new Iraqi defence force that was being hurriedly formed and deployed to get US troops out of harm's way. Bremer and Kimmitt were able to point to these forces and note that Iraqis were sharing the responsibility for Iraqi security. In general the Kurds were loyal to the US, seeing the war as a much-desired liberation for their people. In Baghdad, however, their deployment made many locals resentful.

Mohammed's attitude made things worse, and it took some time before we were allowed to leave the checkpoint. For a moment I was even worried that he and I might be arrested. The Kurds made no attempt to hide their hatred of the people they were searching. 'Idiots, they think the people who fired the rockets would still be here? They left hours ago,' said Mohammed as we left.

# ABU GHRAIB

The next morning I drove out to the prison at Abu Ghraib. It was windy there, and the dust stung my face and made me squint. The prison is about twenty kilometres west of Baghdad on the main highway that runs through Falluja and then on to the border with Jordan.

At the gate a crowd was lined up along paths with walls made of razor wire and dirt-filled wire blast buckets. It was a Monday – the day, I had been told, when very limited visits were allowed to those in the prison for criminal matters. Even so, the majority of those waiting were trying to find or see relatives who had not been detained on criminal matters. Most would not get to see anybody or even get an answer to their inquiries.

It wasn't hard to find people to talk to, although an atmosphere of fear and nervousness hovered over the conversations. Many of those waiting wore headscarves to protect themselves against the wind and the dust, and all spoke in low voices as though the US guards in the watchtower above would hear. The first people Salah and I spoke to were from Tikrit. 'Three months my son has been in the prison. The American went to his house and found a machine-gun. They accused him of having ten, but he has only one. He is not resistance. He just graduated this year from college. He is twenty-four years old. Only God knows when he will get out ... There is no mercy with the Americans. They put them in the prison but with no evidence – even the Red Cross cannot come here. Even the UN. I am seeking for someone to help me. The judge and the executor is the same.'

Another man was waiting to see his brother, who he said was blind. His brother had been in the prison for four months. 'At two in the morning they came to the house. Some spies told them to. After a week the US came back and apologised and promised to set him free, [but] that was four months ago [and] they still have him.' This man refused to give his name, but Salah told me he was a Sunni, and also from Tikrit. Most of those outside the jail were Sunnis and most seemed to be from either Tikrit or Falluja, where the insurgency and the US response to it were most fierce.

After I asked the name of one of those talking and he refused to give it, a large man with a scarf around his head stepped forward through the group now gathered around Salah and me. He said his name was Hasan Oudi Jassim and he carefully made me write it down. He was from Mahmoudiya and he had three brothers inside the prison. They had been accused of buying and selling weapons, but when they were raided by US soldiers on 10 January 2004, only one weapon was found in their possession – a normal state of affairs in Iraq. Jassim said the Iraqi translators working with the US soldiers had stolen money from his house, and two days after arresting his brothers the troops had returned and seized all of their identification. He knew his brothers were in Abu Ghraib – some people who had been released had seen them – although the authorities claimed otherwise.

He moved on to the situation of women held in the Abu Ghraib prison. 'Some people told me they saw the women being treated badly. Some prisoners heard the women shouting all the night,' he said. Everybody else in the small group began to talk about the topic in hushed tones. One man pushed himself forward and spoke urgently to Salah above the others. 'They picked the very religious people and took them and forced them to make love with the US soldiers. There is many talk of this situation,' he said and pointed to the houses behind the prison. 'All night they hear the shouting,' he said. The same man kept talking: 'American law can cover all the situations. The US talk about human rights and all the technology. This means nothing with their behaviour. The fact is they have the technology, but they are depending on the spies and the traitors to rule.' He went on to say that if the US went to arrest someone and the person wasn't there, they would take the girls and the women. I'd heard the same thing said in Falluja.

To the US military it was just standard practice, but to these people it was kidnapping.

What my new informant said next made me doubt his credibility: 'I see American bodies thrown in the river. They drop them from helicopters in Habbaniya Lake three months ago.' I had heard this story elsewhere and thought it implausible that the US forces were trying to hide their war dead by throwing their bodies in a lake.

Another man now handed me a note written in bad English. It said 'Four brothers missing on 2/5/2003' and gave their names: 'Ahmed Ali, Amer Ali, Muhammad Ali and Nidam Ali from the village in the area of Al-Eskandira'. He told his story. He had been given the registration number of one of the brothers and had travelled to the prison in Umm Qasr near Basra in order to see him. It turned out to be the wrong man. 'After that I have looked in every prison in Iraq and I haven't found them anywhere,' said the man, Isa Abdullah, a cousin of the four men. The only way to track someone in detention was by obtaining their registration number. The prisoners couldn't be tracked in the US system by their names. Two men told me similar stories of misidentification and endless searching and frustration.

The man who had told me about the women and the dead US soldiers started to speak again. 'If anybody moves during the night in this area, the American soldiers shoot them,' he said. 'There is an eyewitness, a farmer carrying vegetables at a US checkpoint. They put a bag on his head and searched the car. They searched him again and found some TNT. They put it there. Then they released him ... It is very bad around here. Be careful. Two months ago a Palestinian cameraman was killed here. From al-Jazeera.'

He had been hanging around listening while the others spoke and now he wanted to say more. 'Some women in the prison, they send paper to relatives looking for mercy because the American soldiers fuck them in the prison.' I asked when this had happened, and he replied instantly, twenty days ago. 'Someone was killed by the US soldiers on the other side,' he said, pointing to the back of the prison. 'Fifteen days ago. 10.30 at night. They take the body and the car and put it inside the prison.' I asked him for the names of the women who had sent the note or the name of the person killed as he drove past the back of the prison, but the man wouldn't tell me any more. Nor would he give me his name. I began to think that he was some kind of crank, who was trying to outdo the others with his stories.

We were interrupted by the arrival of a loud group of Iranians. A woman from the group fell to the ground in front of me and began weeping loudly, saying, 'He is my only son.' She had perhaps mistaken me for some kind of official. The story was quite straightforward. Her son had come from Iran as a pilgrim to Karbala and Najaf, but he had been arrested by the Americans in Baghdad with two others. The others had been released but not her son. According to her, he had been arrested after hiring a taxi in Baghdad which had been in an accident and then turned out to be a stolen vehicle. Ironically the driver of the taxi had been set free but this woman's son, apparently only fifteen years old, had been sent to Abu Ghraib. It sounded like a mistake, but with the law courts not functioning there was no way to sort out the mess. The boy didn't speak Arabic and had probably been set up, but of course the US soldiers who arrested him had no Farsi translator on-hand to sort out the problem. Who really knew what had happened? The woman was weeping and telling me she had eight daughters but only one son and she had travelled all the way from Iran to get him. The Iraqis listening to the story showed little sympathy. They had their own problems.

I wrote down a number of other testimonies. All nine male relatives of one man had been arrested on 10 October 2003 at his house in Balad. He said spies had told the Americans to arrest them and they were still in the prison. 'More people in the prison will only make us resist the Americans. All these families will just hate the Americans like in 1917 [when] the British do the same.' A man from Zaba said he had been told that his brother, a doctor, was al-Qaeda and would be released on 1 May 2005.

Another man said he had been released last month after being in the prison for eight months. 'They attack us with wild dogs. One of these dogs bite me on my nose. In June, July, August the treatment was not so bad. In December there is a sudden change with their behaviour.

The same police and old Iraqi Army members learn from the Americans. Maybe the Israelis teach them. The American army does the same thing as them.'

By this time we had attracted a crowd, and we were still standing outside the main gate. Suddenly the old man from Balad told me to hide my notebook and everybody hastily looked at the ground and took a few steps back. I turned around and two US soldiers were standing directly behind me, scanning the crowd. Both had weapons in their hands and one was talking into the headset in front of his mouth. I thought of stepping forward and introducing myself, but the atmosphere was so tense and the soldiers so obviously on alert in a hostile crowd that I just slid my notebook into my pocket and backed away through the crowd with Salah. The people gave no sign that they had been talking to me or that I was a journalist, and the American troops were still standing in the now-silent crowd when Salah and I reached our car. 'You almost got a good story,' said Salah laughing. What, I asked. 'First reporter in Abu Ghraib.' He thought it was very funny.

\*

Back in Baghdad I checked whether any Palestinian journalists had been killed near Abu Ghraib. Sure enough, Mazen Dana, a 43-year-old Palestinian cameraman working for Reuters, had been killed outside the prison on 17 August 2003 by US troops who fired on him from a tank. The US forces later said they had thought his camera was a rocket-propelled grenade launcher. Journalists with him at the time said the US troops were aware of the news-crew's presence and fired deliberately. The matter didn't go any further. The man at the prison had been partially right about that.

The stories I had heard outside Abu Ghraib that morning describing sexual and physical abuse of prisoners would, I felt, be difficult to verify immediately. Although there was a widespread perception among journalists in Baghdad that something very wrong was happening to the detainees, at the same time many were ready to dismiss these 'stories' as just that – inventions designed to discredit the Americans. Most journalists considered the sources of the abuse stories to be enemy combatants trafficking in disinformation. There was also the fundamental patriotism of most American journalists, which prevented them seeing what was happening.

On another level, journalists didn't question Iraqis who had been detained. In fact they rarely met them, due to the gulf between the foreigners and the local people. The ever-worsening security situation kept most foreigners in the isolation of the well-fortified hotels or the Green Zone. The high cost of keeping journalists in Baghdad meant that most permanent correspondents were American, and many of those working for big networks were under very strict security guidelines. CNN reporters, for example, were forbidden to leave their hotels after 4 p.m., following an attack on one of their vehicles which left two of their local staff dead. On the Iraqi side there was the fear that material given to reporters would be passed on to the Americans and they would be arrested again. There was also an understandable reluctance to approach Coalition establishments or the main hotels to contact journalists because all of these buildings were guarded by the same US troops that had abused them.

For their part, the *Time* journalists I knew were also trying to get into Abu Ghraib through the Iraqi justice ministry. But like me they weren't getting anywhere.

*

In the predominantly Sunni suburb of Adhamiya in Baghdad, locals claimed that a third of all men in the area had been detained at some stage in the ten months since the resistance had begun. In the main street, shops were burnt out and bullet-holes from vehicle-mounted machine-guns criss-crossed the upper levels of the buildings where US soldiers had fired in response to attacks on their vehicles as they drove through. On the walls were slogans in Arabic: 'Their tanks are our training for the mujahideen' and 'Jihad is our way'.

We parked and walked over to the main Sunni mosque. I had been told that a local businessman who supported this mosque had had a quarter of a million dollars in US currency taken from his house by US troops during a 'cordon-and-search' operation. I had by now heard many similar stories of gold and money going missing in raids, including from fixers and translators employed by *Time* magazine. It was an almost universal complaint among those who had been arrested. The soldiers always stole whatever money they came across. The sums involved could sometimes be substantial.

The imam was not in and the man in charge of the gate at the mosque had no idea who the businessman in question was. Instead he gave us directions to a local man who had also lost money in raids in the area. The raids were very common due to the constant attacks on US forces in the suburb.

We walked down the main street and into a nearby alley. The man we were looking for was a local carpenter, and we found him in his small workshop, where he immediately produced some flimsy plastic chairs and sent his small son to go and get us some soft drinks. We sat down surrounded by the wood shavings of the workshop. His name was Sahab Ahmed Ali and he told us that on 15 June 2003, at 2.30 in the morning, US troops had raided his nearby house and arrested him, his father and his two brothers. The treatment was standard. They tied their hands and covered their heads with a bag. The troops searched the house for weapons but all they found was eight and a half million dinars and some gold. The sum amounted to more than US$10,000. He was released a month later, as were his brothers and his father. After his release he enquired about the missing money and was told to go to the prison in Basra. There he was told to go back to Adhamiya and talk to the unit that had arrested him. He showed me all the official forms and statements he had filled out and delivered to various offices and bases in the country. He said he had tried a total of thirteen times to get his money back. Finally he was told to lodge his claim with the 3rd Infantry Division in Baghdad who, according to his release form, were the soldiers who had arrested him. But the 3rd Infantry Division had already left Baghdad by then, after being rotated out of the country.

Sahab said he was only one of three people arrested in the same raid who lost money from their houses when they were searched. Another Adhamiya businessman, Maitham Shah Achmed, lost US$45,000 from his house. During his arrest his mother saw the US troops taking the money. When she asked if it would be returned, the US soldier simply told her it was 'dirty money' and it was being confiscated. Maitham was released with no charge ever being laid, but the money was not returned. Unlike Sahab he had not tried to get the money back, regarding it as 'the price of his freedom'.

It is common for Iraqi civilians to keep cash or gold in their houses. With no functioning banking system in Iraq, they have little choice in the matter. 'You have to keep this in your house for everyday expenses, especially if you are in business,' said Sahab. Like most released detainees, he blamed spies who worked for the Americans for his arrest. He said they directed the troops to the houses on raids. Sahab believed the confiscated money was used to pay these spies or kept by the US soldiers themselves.

A week later I finally succeeded in arranging a meeting with the lawyer at the Iraq Ministry of Human Rights. The ministry had been set up by the Coalition Provisional Authority primarily to document the crimes of the former regime. I spoke for a long time with the deputy director about these before asking about the current complaints against Coalition troops, which it was also now handling. Finally, after I insisted that we discuss these complaints, he reluctantly summoned Saad Zultan, the man in charge of this area. I asked him about the most common allegations against the Coalition, and the deputy director looked very uncomfortable as his subordinate answered. The latest allegation he had received about stolen money was two days before and it concerned theft of money by US troops during a raid in Baghdad. Such complaints were 'a daily thing', he said, as were claims by those shot when the Coalition troops opened fire after an attack on them. 'The major problems are the prisoners, damages to vehicles and stealing from the houses,' he said. One case he was handling involved the arrest of a merchant in Tikrit who had lost the equivalent of US$20,000. When he complained about this, he was arrested again. Another case involved the director of an Iraqi newspaper, Mahdi Abul Mahdi, who was arrested in July 2003. All of the newspaper's computers were confiscated and US$10,000 was taken. The Coalition authorities denied that they even had the newspaperman in custody. Zultan said there was not much legal room for pursuing such cases at the moment: 'By order of Bremer we don't have the capability to follow up cases against the Coalition.' He added that he hoped this would change after the 30 June transfer of sovereignty. That, he said, was his main reason for collecting evidence. He added that the Coalition had finally allowed the ministry to set up an office with two lawyers inside Abu Ghraib prison to help sort through the allegations of missing people, but the start date for the office was being continually postponed by the authorities. 'We have a shortage of information. Even those who die in prison, we don't know where the bodies are. They get sick, we don't know where they are sent.' The deputy director was looking very put out by this conversation and the lawyer excused himself. We arranged a time to meet the following week, but when I returned to the ministry I was told he wasn't there and was not allowed to enter the building.

It was a similar story with the Civil-Military Operations Centers (CMOC) responsible for locating detainees and organising compensation claims. The person in charge of them, an Iraqi woman called Zeena, had her office in the basement of the Conference Center in the Green Zone. Zeena, I hoped, could shed more light on what was happening to the detainees. As soon as I sat down in her office, a burly American woman in military uniform joined us. It was Brigadier General Janis Karpinski, who until recently had been in charge of the troops at the prison in Abu Ghraib. She joked that Zeena was becoming a celebrity with the media, because all enquiries to the staff of the assistance centres were invariably bounced up to her. The staff at the branch offices were reluctant to be quoted, and admitted they had been told not to deal directly with reporters. Karpinski now explained that Zeena was too busy to talk to me, and I would have to make an appointment. As I ran through some possible times, Karpinski kept interrupting to say that the suggested date was impossible. Eventually we settled on the following Thursday, but as Karpinski walked me out of the office she told me that I couldn't photograph Zeena for her own safety and that she would have to be present at the meeting. It was clear that I was not going to be allowed to speak to Zeena alone and that the presence of Karpinski, basically her employer and minder, would effectively prevent her talking freely about conditions in Abu Ghraib. I decided the story of Abu Ghraib could wait until I had more material. I needed more solid evidence to break such a story. Although I had no doubt abuses were occurring, the only supporting evidence I had were the Iraqi testimonies that other journalists had poured scorn on. I decided it was time to get out of town again and asked Salah if he would catch the train to Basra with me.

# LAST STOP ON THE ORIENT EXPRESS

Baghdad's main railway station, a well-preserved, British-built edifice, was virtually empty on the morning of my journey. The sole occupant of the domed booking hall was a Shiite woman covered in full-length black who was slowly mopping the marble floor in concentric circles. She told us that there was indeed a train to Basra and directed us to a small window where, miraculously, a ticket-seller was to be found. A first-class ticket to Basra cost little more than one American dollar for the twelve-hour trip.

This had once been the final stop on the Orient Express. The station hadn't been bombed, and there were still signs in English for the 'international travellers waiting lounge', as well as signs to Istanbul and one for 'European travellers'. Although that had all ended a long time ago, it was still a quintessentially British station, with long platforms and small green guard boxes on the platforms. There was hardly anyone around and the train was due to leave in less than half an hour. It was not a good sign.

The carriages were already on the platform and we climbed aboard. A cloud of dust from the ventilation filled the compartments as the train started moving, exactly on time. The windows in the corridor were full of bullet-holes and the cushions of the seats inside the first-class compartments had been removed, leaving just the green vinyl on the hard wood beneath. Most of the fold-down bunks had also been removed, but some still hung on their hinges. Each compartment still had a small plastic intercom with five music options that had long since ceased to function. Salah was aghast. 'This is worse than I thought,' was all he said, but I could tell he was worried. No other passengers were in the carriage and we chose the best of the dilapidated compartments. More staff were on the platform organising the four-carriage train's departure than there were passengers. As the train moved slowly out of the station, everything inside was already coated in a fine brown dust.

The train creaked slowly through the back streets of Baghdad, through scenery of junk-filled vacant lots and piles of burning rubbish tended by children. At a road crossing the cars ignored the slowly approaching train and continued to cross the rails until it was almost upon them. At one road a US Army Humvee prevented the traffic from moving forward. Towards the outskirts of the city destroyed anti-aircraft guns lay by the rail-way and, in one stretch, almost twenty destroyed Iraqi armoured vehicles mouldered in a grove of date palms where they had tried to hide from air attacks as the Coalition forces approached Baghdad almost exactly one year before.

On the railway siding outside Baghdad sat the remains of trains blasted apart and riddled with shellfire in the war. Further along there were locomotives crushed from more recent impacts and passenger carriages gutted by fire and derailed, leaning off the sidings.

When I had asked about the train a few days before, the off-duty guards at the station had assured me that the passenger trains were safe. The goods trains were another story. At least twice a month, they said, the train to Basra was attacked, as were about 80 per cent of the goods trains in other parts of the country. 'The main aim for the resistance is to attack or steal the military cargo,' said Ali Jabar Murad, one of the guards. He told me he had been attacked just last week. 'They remove the railway tracks and force us to stop. Then they steal the goods. There are only two of us [guards]. They have RPGs. I only have an AK47 with sixty bullets. The goods are for the Americans. Why are we suffering for the goods for the Americans?' He told me about a recent incident in which the guards had fired back. The attackers had simply waited until they ran out of ammunition and then come and broken their legs with rifle butts. Another guard, Jusin Alwan, said, 'I only get 300,000 dinars a month. I am not going to lose my life for that.' According to these two guards the goods stolen ranged from computers to weapons to uniforms. 'In Nasiriya at the train station the guards have American uniforms. They stole a whole container full of uniforms from the train,' said Ali. 'If the Americans want the goods to reach Baghdad, they must guard them themselves,' he continued. 'There is no communication. If something happens, we can't let them know.' The guards were laughing. They didn't really care whether the train was robbed or not. It wasn't their problem – they just wanted to get paid. One of them said that he had a PhD in accountancy, but when he had applied for this job they had only asked if he had a primary school education. They told us the passenger train would be fine. There was nothing to rob.

Basra is 550 kilometres south of Baghdad. The train ran through predominantly Shiite areas and only briefly through the so-called Sunni triangle where most of the attacks against Coalition forces were taking place at that time. From the train we could occasionally see convoys of semi-trailers escorted by US Humvees. Aside from that there was no sign of Coalition forces except for one lone patrol of two vehicles sighted in the desert past Samawa much later in the day. The Polish force had responsibility for Hilla along with small numbers of Filipinos, Rumanians and Lithuanians, but their base was on the other side of town near the ruins of old Babylon. The Spanish force had responsibility for the next region further south near Nasiriya before the British-run sector began near Amara. All the forces were on high security alert and never left their bases unless in sufficient numbers to deal with any potential threat. Although there were fewer attacks on Coalition forces south of Baghdad than in the Sunni areas, they still occurred. Bombings such as the car bomb attack on the Polish base in Hilla on 18 February 2004 that killed eighteen Iraqis and wounded sixty-four people including soldiers from Poland, Hungary, the Philippines and an American, were a constant threat.

The trip was oddly peaceful. The train rolled along slowly through the day, past the cultivated areas around Hilla and down to Diwaniya, then through to the drier areas beyond where Saddam had drained the marshes after the first Gulf War to ensure the Shiite Marsh Arabs wouldn't rise up again. It was almost relaxing, but I could see that every time the train stopped Salah would become alert and watch the corridor to see who got on. On the train there was no security. Four policeman were assigned to the train, but they, other passengers told us, had hidden their weapons and wore civilian clothes. When asked what would happen if there was an attack, the group of passengers we were speaking to erupted in laughter. They said the police would probably run away. Further south more passengers boarded the train. They were too poor to travel by car or lived in the areas we were passing through where no roads ran close to the rail line. Our only security lay in the fact that the slow passenger train was not a target of the resistance. Coalition forces wouldn't even patrol the railway, let alone ride on the train.

As we entered the area that had once been marshes but was now just a grey dusty plain with occasional irrigation canals dug into it that flowed with grey, silted-up water, we started up a conversation with Assad Nasser. It so happened that he was the chief inspector of the railways in the south. He had worked for the Iraqi railways for thirty-seven years and was returning to Basra after attending a meeting in Baghdad in which the main problem discussed was last month's unpaid wages from the Coalition Provisional Authority. He was wearing the simple floor-length shirt that is popular in the south and complained about the appalling state of the railways that he had spent all his adult life working on. He sat down in our compartment with another man who was a ticket inspector who had also worked on the trains for many years. When we asked, they detailed fourteen major accidents involving loss of life on Iraqi railways since the previous May when the trains had started running again. It was a long discussion as they ran through all the relevant incidents and decided only to include serious accidents that had killed people in their total. But we had hours to kill as the train slowly rolled south and occasionally slowed to a near stop where the driver knew there was a fault in the line, and we would hear a massive metallic clunk as the wheels passed over it.

Collisions were common, along with deliberate derailing and gunfire attacks. 'Before there was control between the two stations. You would know the line was clear. Now no red light, no green light, no phones, no stationmaster,' said Assad. He said most of the stations in the south had been bombed during the war and the others had been looted. He blamed the Coalition for starting the system again to move cargo from Basra to Baghdad before anything had been repaired. He said that the Coalition refused to guard the stations in the desert and no electricity or food was available out there. The remote stations in the south had been attacked so often that they had been forced to abandon them. He pointed to a looted station as we went past without stopping. There was washing drying on a line and children on the platform. A family had moved in and Assad said if they tried to move the stationmaster back into the station the family would shoot him. The last serious accident on the Basra line had been a head-on collision two weeks before. Both trains had been told the line was clear and the driver and engineer of each had died. The smashed trains had only been hauled off to the sidings outside of Baghdad a few days before where they joined the other wrecks we had passed earlier in the day.

Further south the landscape of the marshes was slowly coming back to life with the gradual re-flooding of the area. Many of the inhabitants had gone as refugees to Iran throughout the '90s to escape the repression of Saddam and the loss of their livelihoods as the marshes dried up. Since the end of the regime they had begun to return, and the train running through this area was one of their few sources of income. In January 2004 the last major attack on this line occurred with the derailing of a goods train. The Marsh Arabs simply removed the tracks, said Assad. When the train tipped over, killing the engineer and wounding the assistant, the teams of thieves got to work opening the shipping containers with welding equipment powered by portable generators and loading the goods onto waiting trucks. When the British forces finally arrived, they took the wounded engineer to hospital but did not interfere with the well-organised thieves. Assad went on to tell a story about his brief stint as a stationmaster at a desert station, where he had been forced at gunpoint by gangs of thieves to tell them which trains were carrying valuable goods.

The train stopped at a desert station. It was not much to see, just a few low-roofed buildings and a small crowd of people coming out to meet the train. There were no signs of any vehicles or roads. It was getting towards dusk and as the light was good I decided to take some photos. I wanted to get a picture of the dilapidated train in the desert, thinking that it could perhaps form part of a deranged travel feature story. As soon as I jumped to the ground, people began to stare and it didn't take too long before I was surrounded by a group of aggressive children and young men yelling and trying to grab my camera. It became slightly threatening and I retreated onto the train. A crowd of young men followed me and stood at the door to our compartment. They were urging each other on and one came and sat down and took the bottle of water on the seat. Salah handled it well, explaining that I was not a spy and that I was not from the Coalition. The young men were intrigued and wanted my camera. Salah told me to put it away. They were just thieves, he said, and referred to them as 'Indians' in English under his breath. Eventually the train inspector came back and sat in the compartment. He told the boy who had taken the water to take his feet off the seat, which he did, and lots of shouting and laughter came from the corridor. The inspector told us there had been problems in this area; some of these boys had been employed as security for the train but there had been many robberies and they had been sacked. He started gently arguing with them and they eventually went away. The natural authority of Salah and the inspector had prevailed. They had wanted to steal my bag and my camera. 'They have never seen a foreigner on the train before. The only foreigners they have seen around here have been soldiers. Most of those children have never been to school. They cannot read and write,' said the inspector by way of explanation. Salah added that he had been explaining to them what a journalist does, but derisively said that these 'Indians' had no idea. As the train finally pulled out of the station and the young men ran out and jumped from the moving train, the inspector said that the only reason they stopped at that particular station was because the local people needed the train and had threatened to shoot the driver if the train didn't stop regularly.

The inspector spoke bitterly of the state of the trains. The carriages we were travelling in had been bought from the French in 1984. They were the height of luxury then and he had personally gone to France to receive training in their maintenance but things had gone down-hill ever since. 'There were no more spare parts in the embargo. We renovated and serviced them, but officially we should not be using these.' He looked around the dusty wrecked interior of the 'first-class' compartment and said, 'The passenger trains are not fit for people, they are not fit for human travel. Wars, occupation, embar-goes, they ruined it.' Once, he said, the trains had fifteen carriages and there were three or four passenger trains a day. 'We used to have restaurants and bars on the train. Sometimes people would just get on to drink at the bar.' In those days the service to Basra took seven hours, now it took twelve. The line had been bombed many times in the Iran–Iraq war, but they had always managed to keep the line open. As it got dark, the flickering lights in the train refused to stay on and we headed south into the marshes in almost total darkness. Outside the occasional shipping container on its side or a derailed flat car or oil tanker showed where ambushes had taken place. When the Coalition had restarted the train service in May 2003, Assad told me, journalists had been invited to cover the first train since the end of the war. He laughed as he recalled the closing shot of the subsequent television report, which had shown the train moving off with everybody waving happily. 'After about two months the thieves started, the derailings, the attacks, the accidents. We should be running seven trains a day but we can't, due to security. Now we just have one for passengers, one for oil and one for goods.' He was sure no other journalists had caught the train since then. In fact, no foreigners at all. We were still talking when we began to pass the burning oil wells in the desert outside Basra which lit the whole area at night. He lived in Basra where he said 65 per cent of the people followed the Shiite cleric Moqutada al-Sadr. As the train pulled into the small station and we got up to leave, he said, 'If he says fight the British and the US, we are ready.'

# BASRA

Basra at night seemed far more relaxed than Baghdad. There were people in the streets, and shops and restaurants open. The military presence seemed much less intrusive and we saw no British troops, although our cab driver said that some Kurds had been arrested while trying to plant car bombs the day before. I'd been told to stay at the Al-Zeiytoun Hotel in the centre of town, but it was full and we found another hotel nearby instead. All the doors of the rooms were marked with the logos of different NGOs and aid organisations that had arrived from Kuwait in the first rush after the war. They had all since departed as the security situation deteriorated. I later found out that almost all foreigners still resident in Basra now stayed in the main British compound outside town at the old airport. The hotel seemed to be suffering. Prices were expensive and in English, and the bored staff outnumbered the guests in the restaurant. There was one other foreign guest, a lanky American 'businessman' with a military bearing who was in deep discussion with some Iraqi men. He ignored my greeting and was gone in the morning.

In Baghdad I had heard often that the situation was more secure in the south of Iraq, where the British were in control. Other journalists even wondered why I was going to Basra, as there was little to report. Iraqis like the translator Omar at the *Time* house told me to watch out for Iranians. They spoke of a grand conspiracy by Iran to take away the south of Iraq and set up a Shiite state along the lines of those presided over by the ayatollahs. Iraqis expressing these sentiments had spent a few years of their adult lives at war with Iran, so it was understandable that there would be residual hate. I wanted to get a feel for what was meant by 'quiet' in Iraq and not hear it from a Coalition spokesperson. That was one of the reasons I made the police my first stop.

Next morning I visited Colonel Noori al-Fayez, a local police commander. Over tea he explained that he was responsible for the northern part of Basra and the main highway as far as Amara. 'I don't want to say this is perfect. There are some incidents, but Iraq is under occupation. It is a mess,' he began. When we arrived, he was sitting at his bare desk in his second-floor office overlooking the street, handwriting receipts. There wasn't much in his office, just the desk and a pile of papers – no computer, no radio. 'Through the work in this sector we have interviews with the criminals. They fit three categories. First they are jobless, second they are using drugs, and third they are the criminals set free by Saddam. It is a big problem for us to deal with all this. We are doing the work of police, military and intelligence with no equipment or weapons. We can't control the area successfully.' He pulled out a table of crimes for the last two months. There were columns for robberies, kidnappings, car-jackings and killings. 'I am trying a new way to get a relationship with the Ashira [prominent families] so they don't fight the police. I am trying to contact some of the imams to preach about the rules. If we arrest one of [these families'] criminals, his family goes and kills the police.' He had lost ten officers in revenge killings following arrests in the last three months. Recently, however, the revenge killings had almost stopped after the Chief of Police in Basra told the Ashira that if any more police were killed, revenge would be taken in kind.

The line between terrorism – as the Coalition and the Iraqis working for them called the attacks – and crime and lawlessness in Basra was a hazy one. 'We have the poorly educated people who see freedom and democracy as killing without being punished ... Some terrorists ... do come from outside Iraq, but we also [have the] Fedayeen Saddam [Saddam loyalists formed or forced into militia before the war in 2003].' Four days before, some Iraqis had been caught by the British with a bomb in their car as they queued for fuel at the busy local gas station. In another incident only two days previously, six Kurds and some Iranians had been detained by the police after suspicious civilians accused them of planning bombings.

According to the colonel, they had since been released, but the incident showed how alert the community was to the threat of people from outside trying to cause problems in Basra. Since the first of Muharram until the tenth, he said, 15,000 police had patrolled the streets of Basra, especially in those areas where religious cere-monies were taking place. Many local people had also armed themselves and patrolled their areas following rumours of the impending arrival of 1500 armed out-siders. Some of these outsiders were captured, he said, but they were not serious terrorists and were released. He said the police had since convinced the people to put their guns away, but added that the religious organisa-tions in Basra were well co-ordinated and well educated and in many cases lent support to the police. Apparently some al-Qaeda members had been captured in Basra in January. An Islamic organisation called Thur Allah (Revenge of God) had been responsible for their capture. The colonel said it was a secret that this organisation worked with the police, but he would call to arrange for me to see them if I was interested. I agreed, and he made the call and sent us off to their headquarters with a policeman as an escort.

Thur Allah were based in an old double-storey Iraqi government building with a few smashed windows and a bare foyer. We were directed to wait in a bare room upstairs with two grubby couches and a desk. One of the men present explained that we were waiting for the leader of the organisation, Said Youssef, who would be arriving soon. In the meantime the men told us about the time they had spent in Saddam's prisons. Their organisation had been formed in 1995 after the first Gulf War and had been involved in the attempted assassination of Mohammed Hamza, the second-in-charge of the Baathist security apparatus at the time. Hamza was one of those responsible for the massacres of Shiites near Basra and in the marshes as their uprising was crushed. In early 1995 Thur Allah attacked the Baath Party headquarters and the Ministry of Industry. After the assassination attempt nearly all of those involved were captured and imprisoned. 'A small cup of soup for ten prisoners in the morning and in the evening one cup of soup and some bad bread,' said one man who had been in prison for seven months from the end of 1999 until 2000. The security forces had accused him of being part of this organisation, but the man said he had not talked and they had released him. He added that their leader, Said Youssef, was in the prison at the same time. After the regime was destroyed in 2003, they set up their organisation above ground with their headquarters in Basra and offices in all thirteen of the country's governorates. Although most of their members had spent time either in Saddam's jails or in exile in Iran, they said there was no connection between their organisation and any foreign power – they were 100 per cent Iraqi.

Said Youssef arrived and welcomed us warmly and invited us through to his dark office in the centre of the building. It was well furnished and there was a wide-screen television and several Thuraya handsets on the table. He sat down behind a large desk. He was in his mid-thirties with spectacles and a quick, intelligent face. Despite the warm weather he was dressed in a black sweater and a dark jacket, contrasting strongly with those around him in traditional floor-length shirts. 'Briefly I want to explain that there are a lot of car bombs in Basra. There is a special operation happening here. One merchant imported five cars from the United Arab Emirates. They were already fitted with the bombs. ... The story started with a Fedayeen Saddam. We capture him and he tells us about his experience in the Saad Square operation to attack the British HQ. They had put [the bomb] in a water-tanker, but the British disassembled it.' Following a beating by the Thur Allah people, the man also admitted to involvement in the car-bomb attack in Najaf that had killed the prominent Shiite leader Ayatollah al-Hakim in August 2003. 'He told us they went to Najaf four times. They had police uniforms, IDs, cars, jeeps. They got a pick-up from an Indian in Kuwait who they killed, BMWs. ... They sent this one man to buy a car in Najaf and to be there at a certain time. They give him US$3000. They get in there at 10 a.m., put TNT in and one of them went near the shrine and parked the car at a certain spot ... they park the car, then detonate with a remote.' Youssef told me that the man they had beaten admitted to a kind of co-operation between former Baath Party members and Syrian members of al-Qaeda. He also claimed that some of these Syrians were in Basra working for the British. It was all background to his main contention. What he was implying was that the British were somehow involved in the whole plot. 'We give them the tapes of the man's confession, but they wipe them and then release the men.' Said Youssef believed, and so did his men, that the British were co-operating with the bombers to weaken the Shiite organisations in the south and that they wanted the security situation to deteriorate so they could stay in Iraq longer.

According to Youssef, the men involved in the bombings were still in Iraq, and their families in Basra had been sent money from somebody in Baghdad. He believed they were part of a group of former Baathist military and intelligence officers who were now working with the Saudis to assist the Americans. He said the arrest of Ali al-Tikriti, a former Baathist leader, by the Americans was some kind of cover as he was involved in directing these groups. It was classic conspiracy theory material, and when I pressed him further he became angry. Why would the British collude to bomb them-selves or kill al-Hakim in Najaf, I asked. 'The British are trying to get the Iraqis to start a civil war.' Why? 'So they can win without fighting.' Why are they co-operating with al-Qaeda? 'Al-Qaeda is a British idea ... Wahab was a British spy. Al-Jazeera knows where Bin Laden is, [but] the CIA they don't know? Come on ...' He dismissed the British as 'now just a small village of the United States' and concluded with a ringing endorsement of all sources of opposition to the US occupation, ranging from the moderate al-Sistani to the radical al-Sadr: 'We support them all.' He said they even supported Sunnis who were fighting the occupation. 'I am not waiting for Sistani to give me the word. If there is an attack on Islam, we will support the end of the occupation in Iraq. Freedom. Freedom to live by Islamic rule.' He promised to get me a copy of the man's confession and said that all the material I needed to confirm his story would be there. I agreed to come back in the evening. When we left, Salah commented on how young Youssef was, and asked, 'Where do you think he gets the money for his organisation?' I said I didn't know. 'Iranian intelligence. It has to be,' he said. I wasn't so sure and thought it was his Sunni paranoia breaking through.

*

My next stop was the Basra branch of Moqutada al-Sadr's organisation. After the fall of Saddam, it too had occupied a former government building, which was now bedecked in the black flags of the Shiite mourning period for their founder Hussein. Outside were sullen guards with AK47s and a crowd of people who were trying to get in through the gates. We were led to a small gatehouse just beyond the fence, where a short, heavy-set man in a white turban and cleric's robes was speaking to five men. A policeman was with him. Salah translated for me as the cleric ordered the men to 'go with him and give him whatever assistance the police require to help them in their duties to secure Basra'. All the while the cleric was looking in our direction to make sure we were paying attention. He spoke next in a loud voice to an old woman who was waiting in the guard-house, telling her that everything would be fine and not to worry. I asked Salah what this concerned and he said something about a property dispute, paying more attention to the cup of tea that had just been handed to him.

The cleric introduced himself as Sheikh Abdul Satar al-Moussawi and apologised for making me wait. He said he had so many things to do to help the community here, so many problems. The police had requested the help of his men, and the poor woman needed money as she had been thrown out of her house. This, he assured me, was his organisation's primary function: helping the community. After we introduced ourselves, he told me that al-Sadr had an office in Australia, in Canberra, 'which I believe is your capital'. It was very hard running the organisation in Basra, he noted, as it was a very big base for the al-Sadr organisation. 'Because we talk directly to the people, not the government, we are always very busy. My followers come directly from the people. We have to send more men to the police tonight because they cannot control the situation and seek my help.' He apologised for the fact that he could not speak to us now and told us to come back at 10 p.m. Sheikh Abdul stood and put his arm around me and led me outside and proceeded to explain in a loud voice to all the guards at the gate that we would be coming back at

10 p.m. and we should not be harmed. Then he shook my hand and bowed slightly, and the guards led us back out through the gates.

In the destroyed old-government district of Basra, more offices of Shiite political groups could be found. There was a large compound for the supporters of al-Hakim and another large office for al-Sistani. But by now it was mid-afternoon and things were quiet, so we headed back to our hotel. Later Salah and I walked through the centre of town looking for somewhere to eat. Almost a year after the fighting had finished, the back streets in the centre of town were still covered in pools of raw sewage that stank in the heat. Piles of rubble and garbage had been bulldozed onto the pavement, and the shell of the looted and destroyed Basra Sheraton was the largest building on the skyline. The roads in the area had been blocked with concrete barriers and piles of barbed wire to prevent car bomb attacks on the nearby hotel, but there were no guards around. In our hotel the foyer was empty except for two bored staff. The atmosphere was one of neglect and bored resignation. Nothing was happening, business was bad in this hotel that catered to the foreigners who were now too scared to stay there, and all indications were that things would soon get much worse.

The British military's headquarters in Basra was the old fort overlooking the Shatt al-Arab waterway. Having heard about the more civilised approach of the British to the occupation, I expected a better reception than I had received previously, but it was just the same as dealing with the Americans. We were told to walk back twenty metres from the checkpoint and wait until the press officer was contacted. As we waited, we sat overlooking the waterway on a stone bench in the dead ground between the coils of wire and concrete barriers, while British Land Rovers raced by as fast as they could, zig-zagging through the barriers as though it were a chicane at a racetrack. There was either something going on or they always drove like that, out of boredom. It was calm and cool down by the river, away from the stinking hot, rubbish-filled streets, and I enjoyed just sitting there, looking out over the wide river that is the confluence of both the Tigris and Euphrates before they flow into the Persian Gulf. Eventually the British soldier who had taken my details came and told us to leave. The major we were after was at the base near the airport. We'd have to go there and we had better call first, he said, while acknowledging that the phone most likely would not work. He gave me another number, saying that this too probably wouldn't work at the moment, as they had just changed over the networks.

Our driver was sitting nervously in the car where we had left him. He seemed very happy that we could now leave this place, where he was afraid of being seen. He took us to the telephone exchange so that I could call the base at the airport. Inside the low, one-storey building was a separate counter for international calls, and banks of phone booths on one side. It was all very efficient:

one of the women behind the counter gave out a number, wrote out a small receipt, and when the booth was free you were called up. It reminded me of a phone exchange in India, with the labour-intensive procedures, the dark-panelled wood booths and the atmosphere of something that, if not actually built by the British themselves, was copied from their institutions. We waited and waited and then were called up. Salah was trying to call his wife in Baghdad, and I was trying to call the British mobile of the major at the base. Of course my call didn't get through; all I heard was a hissing sound in the ancient receiver. Salah couldn't get through to Baghdad either. The woman said to wait. We waited, but as we did I watched everyone else: not one person was connected. Not even those waiting for the local call booths, let alone those in the rest-of-Iraq booths or the international booths. Each caller was still getting up, collecting their receipt, sitting down, waiting, smoking, chatting, getting people to come and get them if it was their number being called out and they had wandered outside. But not one person was being connected. I wondered if the girls behind the counter were getting paid, or if they, and everyone else trying to make calls, were just going through the motions as there was nothing else to do. We gave up and left.

I told the driver to go to the airport, but he went instead to the base at the port and insisted it was the airport and dropped me in front of a checkpoint. It was surrounded by bulldozed piles of dirt and rows of wire with a small sandbagged pillbox positioned next to the gate. There was no one around, and I slowly walked up to the pillbox. Two rosy-cheeked British boys who could not have been out of their teens were huddled inside the tiny space with two automatic weapons poking out through the hole. I introduced myself and stooped down and handed in my identification. One of them said, 'I'm awfully sorry, sir, but you seem to be in the wrong place. We don't even have any comms [communication equipment] here, sir, you'll have to go to the airport.' They were very polite and very young and they looked terrified – like terrified animals – in their small, sandbagged hole. I apologised for bothering them and went back to the car and told the driver to take us to the airport.

It was more than twenty kilometres out of town on the highway and he just didn't want to go there late in the day so he had brought us to the port instead. It was just another base to him and he didn't think they would let me in anyway. Irritated, I told him to go and stop wasting our time. He muttered something in Arabic and then sped out of town past the destroyed tanks in the wide flat desert where they had come out to meet the British and be destroyed.

The base itself was still just a low cluster of buildings in the distance when we reached the checkpoint. Iraqi employees were waiting around for lifts back to Basra, and two British soldiers stood on the highway as the first line of security. A heavy machine-gun was positioned to cover the oncoming vehicles. Once again our scared driver parked far away from the checkpoint, a pointless precaution. There was no other reason to be on this exposed side road off the highway, and the ground was so flat and featureless the cars waiting there could be identified for miles around. One of the British soldiers started chatting to me amiably as we waited for an officer to come out. 'Ah, Australia. Bondi Beach. I love it. Best pubs in the world and the women in Sydney – unbelievable, eh? It'd be still warm in Sydney now, wouldn't it?' I began to get annoyed as he told me that he had another four months to go in Basra. His talk was making me wonder what the hell I was doing there. He was making me think of pubs in Sydney and how I would rather be in one of them than here at a checkpoint in the desert, talking to another officer who would soon be trying to get rid of me. We prattled on and then he saw something and said, 'Excuse me, sir, one moment.' Three large four-wheel drives were speeding down the highway and turning in. He started speaking into the microphone around his neck and shouldered his weapon, but seemed to relax again as the vehicles raced up. A short, extremely sunburnt British soldier wearing no shirt under his body-armour vest leapt out of the first vehicle and screamed for the cars to come in behind him and ran straight past the guard. They had been sent out to escort employees from Kellogg, Brown and Root, the Halliburton subsidiary that was contracted to rehabilitate the oilfields near Basra. Although no one would tell me this at the time, two of their Iraqi employees – female laundresses, sisters – had been shot dead in a drive-by shooting on their way back to Basra in a taxi after finishing work. The shooting had taken place only minutes ago further down the highway, but the British soldier neglected to mention this and instead told me to go and wait in my car. There was nothing left to do but go back into town. He wouldn't let me past even the first checkpoint, and the major was still busy.

*

Cars and trucks were lined up outside the petrol station near the Thur Allah office. Among the vehicles were mule-drawn trailers, loading petrol for the street-side sellers, and a few British Land Rovers parked to one side to maintain order. The atmosphere was aggressive, with people yelling and horns blaring. The problem was distribution. Petrol was still very cheap in Iraq, but the authorities hadn't quite mastered the supply process and queues and shortages were common.

Although the promised taped confession hadn't arrived, Said Youssef invited us in to wait and drink tea. He wanted to talk. He hated the British, he likened them to the Baath Party. He had handed over the confessions to the British, but then they had come and raided his offices. He said that aside from the money and the weapons the British confiscated, they took documents he had been collecting which implicated the British in the illegal export of oil. He said they gave permission to certain merchants and made it illegal for others to export oil products. Then there was the scrap metal. 'Fifteen million dollars the price of this steel. There is a mountain on the border with Kuwait. Equipment, tools, truck digging equipment [are] sent to the border, stolen cars from Iraq, a huge parking area full of stolen cars.' If you asked the Coalition authorities, they would have said contracts had been awarded to those companies capable of fulfilling them, and in the end the revenue would be used for the reconstruction of Iraq. But to Said Youssef it was theft: all he saw were the resources in his area being stripped by companies granted permission by authorities outside the country, mostly American.

His litany of complaints continued. 'They use the bullets with two explosions. They are not supposed to be using them.' 'In Hakimiya close to here two months ago they [the British] attacked some families. They stole money and arrested the men.' 'It is very common for them to take the money. One of the translators with the British soldiers says they want him to change Iraqi money to dollars. They told him they stole it from the banks when they get in to Basra. But this is occupation. This is normal. I suspect they will never leave even if there is a prospect to hand over in July. Every day they take 200 to 250 trucks, take caravans, to build this huge base in Nasiriya. They are not planning to leave.' He was a natural leader and had the whole room enthralled as he denounced the British. He had people laughing, then solemnly nodding their heads at his next point.

'America is here to prevent attacks on and secure Israel. There is no human rights, no humanitarianism. One of Bush's statements was, "We are looking for Saddam, we are looking for WMDs, we are looking for the hidden enemy." What does that mean?' He claimed America was not a democracy with its two-party system. That Great Britain was not a democracy and the Governing Council was not a democracy. He said the Governing Council kept pushing the federal solution for Iraq, which only the Kurds favoured. 'Why must Islamic law of 1500 years comply with this new law? We have to follow Islamic law. Islamic law is the best solution for Iraq. America will be ended, history tells us these stories. These great empires get rich and collapse – Germany, Great Britain, maybe one day Kuwait,' he said, laughing. Then he stopped speaking and turned to me and asked me what I thought. I mumbled something inoffensive about human rights being universal. He laughed. 'Ahh, the Australian talks about human rights. Do you know this man's brother drowned on that boat sunk by your navy?' he said, pointing to one of the men in the room. 'Your prime minister, John Howard, kills Iraqi people.' He was referring to the refugee boat that had sunk between Indonesia and Australia in October 2001, drowning 349 Iraqis. At the time the Australian government was pursuing a hardline policy against illegal immigrants, and it had been a minor political scandal in Australia as the government sought to disavow any responsibility for the disaster.

Said Youssef was now revelling in my discomfort. Revealing the hypocrisy of foreigners proved to all of those present how clever he was. 'This man should be allowed to avenge you for his brother. You are the first Australian he has met since his brother died. His brother was trying to escape Saddam, but the Australians killed him.' He was triumphant. I started to explain that many people in Australia opposed the government's refugee policy, just as many people opposed the war in Iraq. But my words sounded hollow, as though I was pleading and lying to save myself. I recall thinking, 'Great, now I am going to be killed thanks to Howard's asylum seeker policy.'

Luckily my explanation was cut short by a series of loud bursts of gunfire. They came either from the British base across the road or from the troops near the petrol station. Everyone agreed they were British in origin – the sound was deeper than that of AK47s. Someone went outside to find out. 'They are shooting at every movement,' Said Youssef said. I was glad the topic had changed. 'Every time it is the same story. They authorise the people to carry a gun, then a few days later they shoot them and apologise.' He was referring to the fact that some Islamic organisations, like the al-Sadr group in Basra, had not been disarmed and were allowed to patrol and secure their own areas. It was the kind of policy that critics of the Americans advanced as evidence that the British were smarter occupiers. They negotiated with local leaders and recognised existing power structures. Basra did seem more stable as a result. But of course there were problems, and the occasional accidental shooting of a guard by jumpy British forces was one of them. Unlike the Americans, the British had tried initially to get the guns out of the community. Youssef told me his group was disarmed along with the Bader brigade forces that had come back from Iran and the followers of al-Hakim, the Supreme Islamic Council of Revolution. But the effort to disarm had stopped after several months, perhaps when the British realised some organisations could be a stabilising influence.

We left without the tape of the confessions, and I wondered whether Youssef had just wanted someone to rail at. But the core part of what he was saying was that al-Qaeda and unreconstructed Baathists were behind the murder of Hakim. The shots had occurred at the petrol station, and when we went past the British had gone and the petrol station was closed. By now our driver was very nervous and would only drive directly back to the centre of town and our empty hotel.

*

We returned to the al-Sadr office the following day in time for a press conference called by the sheikh. With his own men filming his statements on an ancient Beta Cam the al-Sadr leader launched into the main complaints of his organisation. 'The new constitution is signed by twenty-five men [and] is not legal. The 25 million people of Iraq do not agree with this law. Twenty-five million people do not sign this law. The US has a veto over the Governing Council, so no one can give their right opinion,' he declared. He was sitting at a desk with a microphone in front of him and the men with a camera and a tripod. Beside me sat a local Iraqi journalist. Soon a British journalist, working for the *Christian Science Monitor*, arrived too with his translator, followed by a two-man British television crew. Each of us, it was clear, had been promised a private meeting with the sheikh. He had a smirk on his face as if to say, 'See how important I am.'

The law outlined in the interim constitution was not written by the Iraqi people, he said. This was a major sticking point in the eyes of the al-Sadr organisation, as it did not reflect the desire of the Shiites to live under Islamic law. 'The straight line for the Sadr organisation is to make the election now because we have the ability to do this – Iraq has a lot of scientists and educated people inside and outside Iraq. Months ago they could do this ... The government cannot be appointed. It must be elected. The constitution must be written by the people.' It was an opinion expressed often by the Shiites of Iraq. With over 60 per cent of the population, they were constantly calling for elections that, if held fairly, they would stand a good chance of winning. But the kind of government such an election could produce, dominated by Shiite clerics, was acceptable neither to the United States nor to their allies the Kurds and the former exiled elite who controlled the Governing Council.

The British journalist from the *Christian Science Monitor* asked if the al-Sadr organisation would accept a position in the Governing Council. Furthermore, didn't the 30 June handover mean that the Sadr organisation would get its opportunity to take part in the government? The sheikh dismissed the idea: 'It is impossible for us to join a government under the supervision of the Americans.' As for the supposed handover date of 30 June, he laughed as the question was translated to him. 'One day they will leave. One day we will fight against them. But they won't leave on June 30 ... The occupation will never be ended. This occupation was planned for ten years before the war. Iraq is a rich country. The last barrel of oil will always be the end.'

The questioning turned to the disarmament of the al-Mehdi army, the militia of the al-Sadr party. Sheikh Abdul Satar al-Moussawi refused to talk about disarmament. He called the militia a 'natural extension of the population's stand together with the imam [Moqutada al-Sadr] to fill the world with peace and justice. This army wants to serve Islam. Its creation is spiritual. The al-Mehdi army works without payment.' He said the army was not a threat and that the al-Sadr movement had as many as 12 million followers in Iraq. 'Through them [the al-Mehdi army] our followers are gathering with the police helping with security.'

The British journalist's concentration was wavering. Every question was answered in oblique religious phrases. The gulf between the two sides of the room was already widening when the British television journalists asked about the two women who worked for the Coalition who had been killed yesterday. 'The girls were human, but it wasn't the right situation for a woman to work for the Coalition. They shouldn't do this,' said the sheikh. 'So your people killed them?' asked the journalist. 'Maybe the murderers are British or American. Maybe the murderers are from the same tribe,' came his reply. The senior al-Sadr man in Basra was not exactly admitting to the murders, but he was agreeing with them in principle.

The sheikh was now irritated. He wanted nothing further said on the matter. The other British reporter took another line of questioning. He asked about the need for the al-Mehdi army. The sheikh talked in broad terms. The army was not a threat. It stood for peace and justice and legal rights. 'We have had forty years with the Iraqi army. We do things and we are executed or dismissed by them. We are not like them.' But Iraq is building an army – why do you need these militia, the same reporter asked. 'The new Iraqi army is just supervised by the old Americans,' he said, smiling.

Next question: 'The people who sell alcohol. Many are killed. Do you agree with this?' (There had been killings of alcohol sellers in Basra for months now.) 'God not allow this because those that drink alcohol, his mind will be out of control. So we don't need to fight these kinds of crimes, we have to fight the roots. To stop people drinking, we must stop people selling. We start with advice, but then if they disobey we have to execute them,' said the sheikh. The reporter almost yelled, 'Do you give the same warning to the women working with the British Army?' 'Yes, because we are the followers of the prophet Mohammed. We don't let them work. We get information from the officers and even the maids who work there. There is a red line and they crossed the red line. We are Muslims and we don't agree with the women working with the foreigners,' he said. The reporter looked pleased with himself. The television crew began packing up the camera and were smiling and nodding nervously as they exited the room. They had got what they needed. The other British reporter seemed to give up his questioning too. The perception had taken hold that the followers of al-Sadr were so hard-line that they were hardly worth talking to, and the small press conference broke up, much like the previous attempts by the Coalition to deal with al-Sadr.

The interview was more or less over, and we walked outside. Aside from the approval of the killing of the women and the assassination of alcohol sellers in Basra, I thought the sheikh's demands quite reasonable. He was the leader of a community that was finding itself without a role in the new political system being established by the Coalition in Iraq. He was being sidelined from the political process. With no other recourse his followers were preparing to fight while still pushing for elections. The refusal of the Coalition to negotiate with the al-Sadr movement as they continued to call for

Islamic law, immediate elections and the withdrawal of foreign troops only hardened the stance of the movement's leaders. They were being left with no other option than to fight the Coalition, thereby turning what should have been the Americans' natural allies into their enemies. The situation in Basra, I felt, was leading to some sort of confrontation. The Shiites had always been considered allies of the Coalition, but it seemed they felt the time was coming when they would fight. Their acquiescence to the occupation had been taken for granted for too long, and now they wanted their share of power.

*

The Basra Chief of Police, General Mohammed Karlo, did not see the Islamic organisations as a problem. 'I am not afraid of these organisations ... They are Iraqis and they support us.' He said he was more concerned at the fact that the borders were open from every side and they could not control them. The Ashira (the powerful families) were another major problem. 'They have their own law. They have no respect for the policeman.' A further problem, unique to Basra, was how to deal with the Marsh Arabs. 'The people who live in the marshes. When he [Saddam] dries them, they escape to Iran. They come back for revenge. They suffer a lot in the last twenty years and they think that gives them a right. This is a big problem for the police now. These people come in to Basra and Amara, live in government buildings, they take land, acting as criminal now. We can't fight them. They say they lost their lives before. There is no law to deal with these people.'

It had taken me a couple of hours to get to see him. The main police headquarters was a hive of activity and heavily guarded. His office was well appointed, with two-way radios, phones, computer – everything you would expect. He was carrying a pistol and had two bodyguards outside with AK47s. He praised the British for their assistance and training. His force now numbered 9000 and soon he hoped to expand it to a maximum of 12,000. He admitted there was a long way to go to establish law and order in Basra and the reasons were obvious: 'There is an interference between the economy and the society. We are looking forward to meeting these kinds of problems.' He said there were fewer problems with terrorists in Basra than in Baghdad, as they were better able to track foreigners coming in and out. He said they had arrested some Saudis and Syrians. 'The intelligence system is stronger here in Basra, as 90 per cent of the people are Shiite. These foreigners can't get into the streets here. Sometimes we get intelligence about actions and we arrest them beforehand. The foreigners we hand over to the British.' He mentioned that on the day before the interview, 12 March, they had disassembled two bombs in the centre of Basra. He dismissed the case of the two murdered women, saying simply that they had been warned. It was obvious that the police co-operated with the Shiite groups. Later, when these groups took up arms against the Coalition, the police would in general stand by and do nothing. Contrary to his claims, his intelligence network would also be unable to forestall all the bombing attempts. Less than a week later, on 18 March, a bomb would explode outside the Al-Zeiytoun Hotel killing five people, where I had been told to stay. That would be followed on 21 April by three suicide bomb attacks near police stations and an IED attack that killed a total of sixty-eight people and injured more than a hundred.

*

The train departed for Baghdad exactly on time the following morning. Once again the carriages were almost empty and their interiors coated in dust. Outside Basra, derailed oil tankers lay on their sides by the railway. They had been pushed off the tracks to clear the line and were surrounded by large black oil stains in the sand. On a siding in one of the villages in the marshes sat a row of shipping containers on flatcars. Each one had three sides of a square cut with a blowtorch in its side, and the metal had been bent upward, like a door. They were still locked but empty, except for the children standing on top and throwing the occasional stone at the slowly passing train. Eleven hours later, approaching Baghdad, two US helicopters swooped low over the train. They were the first Coalition forces we had seen since leaving Basra. Salah and I left the train in the suburbs and walked off through the deserted railway yards to find a taxi. In the cab on the way to the house, we heard the first of the evening's random explosions and gunfire. The driver shrugged his shoulders and said he didn't know what it was.

# ONE YEAR ON

There was a long line outside the Convention Center on
17 March 2004. The first anniversary of the start of the
war that toppled Saddam Hussein was approaching,
and many news organisations had sent reporters back
to do their one-year-on stories. I was standing in the
queue to get into the Green Zone with many of these
recent returnees. Next to me was a Canadian journalist
from Toronto, who had covered the war last year. He
had flown in that morning and this was his first trip
outside the airport or the heavily fortified hotel. He
asked me if it was safe standing in the long, stationary
line of journalists and Iraqi employees of the CPA that
stretched out past the blast barriers onto the street. It
was a good question. No, it wasn't safe, I replied. As far
as I could tell, it was only a matter of time before such
a prime, regularly stationary target as the queues of
journalists going to briefings would be hit. He wasn't
the only one to see the danger, and it was with relief

that we entered the Green Zone after almost an hour of waiting.

Brigadier General Kimmitt was delivering a background one-year-on briefing designed for those who would be writing the big features for the anniversary. It was supposed to be a case of highlighting the successes and achievements so far, just one short year after the first bombs had been dropped on Baghdad on the night of 19 March 2003. The bombs that marked the start of the war were supposed to have been 'a surgical strike on leadership elements', but they had really been a botched attempt to assassinate Saddam. The intelligence agencies had got it wrong from the start. By the time we made it past the security we were running late, but it didn't matter. The journalists were filing out of the auditorium and sitting on the floor in the foyer in a tight circle around Kimmitt, who was standing and preparing to speak with no microphone. The power had failed just in time for the briefing that was to tell us how much had been achieved.

Kimmitt began with the military operations. 'Since November 15 we have transferred 300,000 Coalition troops in safety with minimum loss of life. [During this time] we didn't stop offensive operations.' He was referring to the rotation of the troops. 'Oil production and the electricity supply have been restored to pre-war levels,' was his next point, which brought snickers from the journalists seated on the floor in front of him straining to hear his unamplified voice. He went on to say that in

October and November they had conducted major operations against 'former regime elements' and were averaging 'fifty contacts a day' with hostile forces. The aim of these operations, he said, had been to kill or capture those responsible for the fighting, but more importantly to get intelligence information on the resistance. The result was the capture of Saddam in December: 'Up to then we were looking at the bottom feeders.' From capturing Saddam, Kimmitt said they had gained a better understanding of the organisation and finances of those they were fighting against. He dwelled on the capture of Saddam, saying it had caused the 'fence sitters' to come over to the Coalition. 'When we picked up Saddam, the hopeful and the fearful were coming over to our side.' He pointed to the two big operations against the resistance that the Coalition had conducted, Iron Hammer and Iron Cyclone, and credited them with reducing the level of contacts to 'about twenty a day'. If you didn't know any better, it sounded as if things were coming under control. Attacks on the Coalition were down and by their reckoning a corner had been turned. I'd heard stories about these operations from those that had covered them. One *Time* photographer said of Operation Iron Hammer that it had involved little more than the use of planes and missiles to blow apart disused warehouses on the outskirts of Baghdad. 'We went out there the next day. There was nothing there in those buildings. They were empty,' she recalled. It did make a lot of noise, though, and could be heard throughout Baghdad.

Iron Cyclone was much the same, but incorporated more cordon-and-search operations, which resulted in more people in Abu Ghraib but little else.

Kimmitt acknowledges a rise in attacks against 'soft targets and Iraqi institutions'. These attacks, he said, were intended to take Iraq 'back to a dictatorship. Back to the seventh century as some extremists would prefer.' He said they were averaging about 'four or five terrorist attacks a month' and these attacks were 'suicidal, spectacular and symbolic'. He mentioned the attack on the army recruitment centre in Iskandiriya. 'Any organisation that is trying to co-operate with the Coalition is a target,' he said. 'These forces are trying to Balkanise the country,' but the Iraqi people had 'used it as an opportunity to pull together'. He said that in the problem towns of Falluja, Baquba and Tikrit, in the Sunni triangle, the number of attacks was down and things were under control. 'The real threat to security is not those elements. Those are hit-and-run tactics.' He pointed to the downward trend in casualty figures for Coalition troops for November, December and January to back up his argument that things were improving.

It was classic Kimmitt. He was stating things in his characteristically earnest, clipped way which gave the impression that he was stating absolute truths. He had a way of looking deadly serious even when saying the most basic things. He dismissed Islamic terrorists as simply wanting to take Iraq back to the seventh century. There was no mention of why they were fighting or what they wanted, such as elections – they were simply lumped in the 'terrorist' category and thus the only thing to do was to 'kill or capture' them. The Coalition's stated belief that they were dealing with either 'former regime elements' or 'terrorists' showed a fundamental misunderstanding of the extent to which ordinary Iraqis were coming to hate the occupying forces due to their routinely heavy-handed behaviour. That hatred was building and would in the coming months burst forth onto the streets with scenes of jubilation when Coalition forces were attacked in Falluja and Americans, in particular, were killed.

Were there any al-Qaeda suspects in detention, Kimmitt was asked. Each time a bomb went off, the Coalition implied that it was the work of al-Qaeda, in particular the mysterious Zarqawi. It was fair to assume that of the 10,000 or so detainees, one at least must be al-Qaeda if there was any truth in what the Coalition said about the attacks. Kimmitt tried a joke: 'We don't have anyone in detention who has a valid membership card for al-Qaeda.' Nobody laughed, and he continued: 'We've seen a couple of other groups, but we don't yet have al-Qaeda members.' The next question concerned the detainees and why they were being held. 'All the detainees we hold are deemed to be a threat to Iraq,' he said. 'We have released 300 and those detainees deemed to be a security threat are roughly around 9500 today.' That was the extent of the official line on detainees at the time. Later, of course, after the evidence of torture emerged, hundreds would be released in large groups as if by decree, in an effort to counter the damage done by the revelations concerning their treatment.

He was asked what guarantees the Coalition could give that the security situation would improve. 'I've got 130,000 guarantees. I've got 200,000 other guarantees in the Iraqi security forces,' came the blithe reply. He was asked when the Coalition was going to leave Iraq. 'The war we conducted was clearly the most precise military action the world has ever seen. Nobody wants to be occupied and nobody wants to be an occupier. The clear consistent message for the people is while we don't want to be an occupier we will not stay here one day longer than necessary and we will not leave one day too soon.' It was the perfect answer to an unanswerable question.

Kimmitt – and the US military more generally – seemed to see the conflict in purely military terms. His one-year-on report made no mention of the effects of US military action on the people of Iraq – the way the behaviour of US troops was provoking such widespread and growing hatred. This didn't seem to fit the equation, had apparently never been considered as a possibility. The US military were the most powerful military force in the world, and there was probably no country in the world that they could not invade and occupy in a few weeks, but that meant little when it came to their larger aim of transforming Iraq into a friendly, functioning democracy.

The topic was raised of last year's looting, which the US forces had stood by and watched. Many ordinary Iraqis believed that the looting had been part of a plan to weaken Iraqi society, to create the conditions for the US to stay longer, to cover up for the crimes the old regime committed in collusion with the Americans, or just to punish the Iraqi people. Almost everybody I spoke to thought it was part of a wider US plan rather than the result of a lack of forward planning. The intact tower blocks of the Oil Ministry, the only government building protected from the looters by the US forces, were always broached as an example by those Iraqis who blamed the looting on the US, saying sagely, 'That shows why they came here – for the oil.' All Kimmitt could really do was try to play it down. 'The looting set us back some measure of time. The copper, the wires, they have to be replaced,' he said. Telephone lines and power lines had been systematically looted to be sold for scrap, mostly by unemployed Iraqis. This had continued for months after the US arrived, with some correspondents telling me that they had still seen buildings being stripped as late as December 2003. 'It was not a great way to start. Had the looting not happened we'd be a long way forward in rebuilding infrastructure.' Then he added, 'There's enough weapons and ammunition in this country. I am not sure the looting changed that much.'

One journalist asked if the celebrations planned for the anniversary of the war would be safe from attack.

Kimmitt couldn't really answer that; he knew full well that the resistance would try to make the most of such an occasion. 'We are looking closely at all aspects of the celebrations. There is no way we are 100 per cent sure there will be no attacks. But that is a fact of life in Madrid. A fact of life in Istanbul,' he said, pointing to two recent sites of terrorist bombings. It was a lame answer, and I looked around to see if any of the other journalists perceived how laughable this attempt was to equate attacks in other countries with the war in Iraq as all part of some kind of global fight. In Baghdad they were occupying a city of five and a half million people and they hadn't even begun to attain a degree of control over what happened outside their own compounds. Nor could they stop their own compounds being regularly attacked by mortars, rockets and suicide bombers. That was a very different reality from life in Madrid and Istanbul. The attempt to compare them merely showed Kimmitt to be an anti-terror zealot or else an accomplished spin doctor. The key message his superiors were giving him was 'link Iraq to the War on Terror' and he was trying to get it in whenever he could.

Finally he was asked if the extra 60 million dollars Bremer had pledged to beef up the security on the borders of Iraq after the Ashoura bombings had made a difference. 'You can build a mile-high wall around this country and the terrorists will still get in.' That was because most of the 'terrorists' already lived in Iraq and were Iraqis. They were fighting the occupation as much for its inability to provide security for, or economic benefits to, anyone but the occupiers themselves. There were foreign fighters among the resistance but, as the Coalition would soon realise, the ordinary Iraqis who were starting to hate the Coalition more and more were the people they would end up fighting, not the nebulous network of foreign terrorists they kept telling us about. But they had to maintain the line, because if they admitted they were fighting ordinary Iraqis it would mean they were fighting those they had saved from Saddam.

*

That night I joined a party of journalists at the Al-Hamra hotel restaurant, the only drinking hole of the foreign press. At our table was a young British freelance cameraman. He hadn't been in Baghdad long and he was shaken and jittery. Only an hour or so before he had been driving down the main street of the Karrada shopping district. The traffic was bad, as it usually was, and his car was barely moving. Then, boom, an IED exploded as a Humvee moved adjacent to it in the traffic. There wasn't much he could do, stuck in traffic; he couldn't leave the scene. Instead he tried to do some filming. He had the nervous hyperactive energy of someone who had just had a life-threatening experience.

While we were talking and drinking, someone came running into the restaurant to say that a huge car bomb had just exploded outside the Mount Lebanon Hotel only a few blocks away. With all of the talking, none of us had heard it. The others went immediately into the foyer and reached for their phones, leaving the table piled with half-finished drinks. I reluctantly followed them. The bombing was already on the television in the reception, and people watched it, crowded around. The al-Jazeera office was virtually across the street from the hotel, and they already had someone there. We watched on television the flames still burning and the street being blocked by Iraqi police. The whole front of the building had been sheared off. The camera crew for the BBC were racing past us out the door carrying their body armour. There were early reports that foreigners were staying in the hotel and that was why it had been targeted. One of those present said he was sure that was where a troupe of British clowns, who had come to Iraq to perform for the underprivileged, were staying. A few bad jokes were made and a few of the journalists, including me, returned to the restaurant to finish their drinks. The British journalist I had been drinking with was leaving the next day and showed no inclination to race down there, even though it was only a few blocks away. Neither did I. He justified his decision by saying that he had already sent his piece for the day and the office would update it with the details of the latest bombings from the wires. I justified it by saying that the correspondent for the papers I was trying to sell to in Australia was here in Baghdad and would undoubtedly write a long, detailed piece. The bombing had occurred between the two hotels where foreign journalists were based in Baghdad, the Al-Hamra and the Palestine/Sheraton compound. The bombsite was therefore almost perfectly placed to be covered by the foreign media who were in town in large numbers doing their anniversary pieces. Suicidal, spectacular and symbolic was what Kimmitt had called the attacks earlier that day, and this one was no exception. The timing was perfect, as was the location; news-crews were doing stand-ups from the bombsite long into the night. I had a nagging feeling that I should have gone down there, and so, I think, did a few of the other reporters. Speaking for myself, I knew what the problem was. I was afraid to see all that again.

Michael Ware wasn't afraid, though. A fellow Australian and friend who worked for *Time* magazine, Ware had spent considerable time on the ground in Baghdad, where he had gained a reputation for courage and good connections. He was the only foreign journalist to have accompanied resistance fighters as they attacked Coalition forces in Iraq in late 2003, which had also made him a figure of some controversy.

By the time I returned to the *Time* house, he had been to the bombsite and was being interviewed by CNN, and then by a host of other networks and radio stations in the US. This is what he told CNN.

MICHAEL WARE, *TIME* CORRESPONDENT: When I approached the scene ... I ... saw the chaos, the pandemonium and the panic. I managed to press through the [unintelligible] and made it through to the bomb crater itself, this massive wound that's been gouged out of the road.

And the thing that most struck me, having been here over a year, is that I have seen this before time and time again. I remember last summer when the Jordanian embassy was hit, the first big suicide-car bombing, closely followed by the UN headquarters bombing. And that's the bombing that this one most closely resembles.

That was 1500 pounds of scrounged ordnance and bombs and artillery rounds. Tonight was 1000 pounds. This might be terrorists doing it, but they can't collect that material without Iraqi logistics support ... The most tragic thing about it is that so far, as much as we're aware, we still have not caught any of these bombers from the Jordan embassy, from the UN headquarters, nor from any of the most recent things. This is a long-term, ongoing campaign, and these guys keep getting away with it and it's only going to escalate.

WOLF BLITZER: *Time* magazine's Michael Ware reporting for us on the phone. Be careful over there, thank you very much for that chilling assessment.

In between interviews he complained that he was being cut off and cut short. He was often asked for comments by the US networks as he was often on the scene and was known to always get close to the action.

But this time he was telling them something they didn't want to hear and it seemed the US networks weren't quite ready for the bad news. His assessment that the Coalition was unable to stop the attacks, or even to find out who was responsible was simply not something that people wanted to hear. The very fact of Iraqi involvement in the bombings was unwelcome news. These things were too much at odds with the official line being faithfully spouted by most other commentators apparently 'on the ground' in Iraq. It wasn't the commentators' fault. They knew no better. On the orders of the so-called security experts employed by their networks, they weren't allowed out very much these days. Nor for that matter were the Coalition spokespeople who gave them information. The resistance campaign was getting stronger and stronger, but the reality of that hadn't yet been acknowledged by the Coalition. Most reporters, myself included, didn't have the depth of experience in Baghdad to see how powerful the insurgents were becoming. Nor was it well-understood that the Coalition – despite its frequent operations – was having little success in capturing or combating them. On the night of the bombing, another such Coalition operation, this one entitled Iron Promise, was taking place. A few days later I spoke to a photographer who had covered part of the operation in the village behind the prison in Abu Ghraib, where attacks were often launched on the walls of the prison with RPGs and small arms. He said not much happened. The troops shot a dog for barking.

The next morning the Governing Council issued a statement on the latest bombing. They condemned the attack and said the victims, which they numbered at twenty dead, had given their lives for the sake of a new and democratic Iraq. They said that 'such acts are probably imported from overseas.' The only people staying at the hotel who had worked in connection with the Coalition were some Egyptian telecommunications company employees. The Governing Council praised the efforts of the Iraqi police and the fire brigade and said they would try to ensure they obtained enough equipment in future to deal with similar incidents. There wasn't much else they could say.

Iraqi ICDC troops stood guard at the entrance to the sealed-off side street where the bomb had gone off. All the buildings around the Mount Lebanon hotel were blackened by fire. Their windows were missing and, in the case of those across the street from the blast, whole sections of front walls and roofs were missing. Cars that had been parked along the street were twisted blackened wrecks; some had been crushed by falling masonry. One was pinned under a pile of rubble. On its front bonnet was a broken child's doll that had fallen from the house above. The house was missing its front walls; on the first floor could be seen the child's bedroom, with brightly coloured prints still fastened to the rear wall even though the blast had taken off the front of the building. As we walked up, an old woman approached Salah. She was a relative of a family that had lived in one of the houses. All dead, she said to him. The entire family had been killed. She wasn't asking him a question, just stating the fact.

The bombing had destroyed both sides of the street. People speculated the Mount Lebanon Hotel hadn't been the target – possibly the suicide bomber's car had just been passing by when the bomb exploded. The car had exploded almost in the centre of the road and not up against the building, which would have been more effective. The bomb crater was now full of water from the fire-hoses, and the whole street was dotted with black pools of water and ash. Television crews with reflector panels to throw light onto their reporter's face were standing in the rubble filming. A few US troops were there, and a Humvee blocked the other end of the side street. Among the crowd were some foreign civilians. They were all young and one was sobbing, with her arm around an Iraqi woman who was also crying. They told me they were part of a Christian peacemaker team that worked with Iraqi organisations to deliver aid. Others, staying around the corner, were members of the troupe of clowns we had joked about. They were earnest people who were in Iraq at their own expense to try to help in some way. These were some of the few foreign humanitarian workers still remaining in Baghdad, but because of their anti-Coalition stance many reporters dismissed them as woolly-headed.

One of those present that day, Jo Wilding, would later show incredible bravery by sneaking into Falluja to

deliver medical aid when it was under siege by the
Marines and reporting on the appalling conditions inside the town. Another colleague of hers, an Australian
woman, Donna Mulhearn, would do the same, and for
her efforts be labelled as irresponsible by the press and
the government in Australia, including by the prime
minister, John Howard. Salah later told me that while
I was talking to them, he had told their Iraqi friend to
stop crying. 'I said to her, if you let yourself cry you will
never stop.'

*

Michael Ware had been back in touch with his contacts
from the resistance and they had given him a DVD they
had made and were distributing. It was a recruitment
tape for one of the many groups fighting the Coalition.
We sat down and watched it. As well as filming their
own attacks with IEDs on a convoy of Humvees, a petrol
tanker and a car, the production included footage showing how the US forces treated the Iraqi people they
detained. It showed hooded prisoners being led away. It
showed those shot by the Coalition with close-ups on
their wounds. It showed blurry footage of US troops
opening fire on a crowd and people running as tracers
flew over their heads. It called on the Iraqi people to join
in the struggle against the Coalition, using the brutality
of the US troops as the emotional trigger to attract people to the struggle. Some of the footage, I think, had
been lifted from news reports. The message was simple:

we have to fight the brutal occupiers, look what they are doing to us.

Michael left that day for Afghanistan, where the US was trying to catch Bin Laden in another operation. I left the same day for Kurdistan. As we made the long, slow drive north on the wide empty freeway in Salah's clapped-out car, I kept seeing the video images of cars and trucks and Humvees exploding from IEDs. It was the suddenness of the explosions that kept coming to mind. There would be lines of cars travelling on a highway through the desert, the appearance of normality, and then one would explode. The attacks had been filmed by those who had placed and detonated the explosions, which meant they were able to capture the precise moment of the explosion on camera. The highway I travelled on to Kirkuk looked exactly the same as those on the DVD, and I was on edge all day.

# GREATER KURDISTAN

It was the Kurdish new year festival, Nawroz. In the rolling green hills to the north of Kirkuk, people had gathered to celebrate, bringing their own tables and chairs. There was dancing and eating in the open air and the atmosphere of a large family picnic. Although the celebrations didn't lend themselves to attacks, the Kurdish authorities were taking no chances and had instituted extensive security checks on all the roads.

We drove further north past Kirkuk to Erbil and were held up in endless rows of vehicles, stretching through the countryside, that recalled the traffic jams at the end of a long weekend. Those manning the roadblocks thoroughly searched all vehicles with Arab passengers. At one, outside Erbil, Salah was marched away by an aggressive Kurdish guard in an American uniform. I could see Salah explaining and pointing to me, and the guard angrily pushing him around and shouting at him in Kurdish. Salah's ID and car registration identified him as a resident of Baghdad, and that was exactly what they were looking for. There had been massive bomb attacks on the offices of the Kurdish Democratic Party (KDP) headquarters and the Patriotic Union of Kurdistan (PUK) office in Erbil on 1 February 2004, and similar attacks were anticipated during the holiday period.

After the first Gulf War, Kurdistan had been placed under the international protection of a no-fly zone, removing this part of Iraq from the control of Saddam. Power in the zone was divided between the two Kurdish political parties, and in the mid-'90s the rivalry between them erupted into full-scale fighting. Now the KDP, under Massoud Barzani, controlled Erbil and the PUK controlled Sulaimaniya.

Kirkuk, however, had remained part of Iraq. Ever since oil was discovered there after World War I, the Kurds had wanted to control it. There are no resources or industries in Kurdistan, and the leaders of the Iraqi Kurds had long dreamed of a separate country funded by the oil deposits of Kirkuk. During World War II the founder of the KDP, Mustafa Barzani, led an uprising which was crushed; it would be the first of many. After another failed uprising in 1969–70, the Iraqi government recognised the Kurds as one of two nationalities in Iraq and recognised the Kurdish language. But the government in Baghdad refused to give the KDP control of Kirkuk, and so the trouble continued. In 1972 the Baath regime nationalised the Iraq Petroleum

Company, making it a core income stream for the country and hardening its resistance to the Kurdish demands.

Complicating all of this was the deep-seated rivalry of the KDP and the PUK, which prevented any cohesive opposition to Saddam. The two groups speak different dialects, Kermanji in the KDP-dominated north and Sourani in the PUK south. They were often rivals in the constantly shifting chess-game of alliances with Iran, Turkey, Syria and the regime in Baghdad. After the 1991 Gulf War, the CIA became involved, and more recently there have been reports of Israeli agents and influence. The principal factors behind the constant outbreaks of fighting between the PUK and the KDP throughout the '90s were money, territory and control of the lucrative taxes at the borders with Turkey and Iran. For many years these taxes have provided the main income for the region. That was why the Kurds wanted Kirkuk, as a replacement source of wealth on which to build a secure nation.

Salah was brought back and made to open the hood of the car and instructed to pull apart the air filter to show that no explosives were inside it. In fact, the car did not even have an air filter; at this point Salah shrugged and told me it had been stolen. The car, it was clear, was near the end of its life. I was realising, too, what a big mistake it was to travel around Kurdistan with an Arab driver who had been a member of Saddam's armed forces.

All the government offices in Erbil were closed for the holiday, their buildings barricaded and surrounded with guards. The streets were almost deserted. In the town's main hotel, heavily armed Western contractors sat around waiting to use the internet. During the war Erbil and Sulaimaniya had been used as bases for the CIA and US special forces as they co-ordinated the entry of the Kurdish forces into Mosul and Kirkuk. Under the occupation they had become secure enclaves for the US authorities to carry on their work building up the Kurdish forces. Many of the armed Western men in civilian clothes waiting in the foyer under the ever-present portraits of Barzani were involved in training and recruiting Kurds for the new national army or for the many security firms contracted by the Coalition to protect oil-related infrastructure near Kirkuk. It was peaceful in Erbil, but it was a heavily armed peace that seemed to require constant vigilance. Besides the Westerners, there were the police, the Iraqi army and many different uniformed security guards and militia on the streets. All of these groups had their origin in the Peshmerga, the Kurdish militia who had fought Saddam – and each other – on and off for the past thirty years.

We drove back to Kirkuk in the dark. Unlike in other parts of Iraq, the biggest danger driving at night here seemed to be drunken Kurdish drivers overtaking at high speed, playing a game of chicken with the oncoming traffic to see who would pull over first. Approaching Kirkuk the huge permanent gas flames from the oil fields lit up the road. There seemed to be many more of these flames than during the day, and I later learned that the local administration had lit the trenches of oil left over from the war as part of the day's celebrations.

Kirkuk itself was quiet, although I noticed US troops standing guard outside the office of the Turkmen National Front. Next morning I went there to find out why. The US guards left us alone as Salah and I introduced ourselves to those in the bare, cramped office. We were shown upstairs, past another US soldier stationed on the landing, to the office of Dr Tallard, the deputy chairman of the Turkmen National Front. Immediately he began to tell us that the Kurds were trying to change the population balance of Kirkuk in their favour. 'The Kurdish people come, they occupy this building, the government buildings, the stadium. All Kurds in the local administration now, in the police force. It is a major problem. That is why the Humvee is outside,' he said. According to Dr Tallard, fifteen young Turkmen men were killed by Kurdish police at a demonstration in January 2004. Then, while the leadership were in Baghdad lobbying for their rights to be included in the transitional constitution, the police (Kurdish) had come to their office on 29 February and smashed everything, including computers and furniture.

Dr Tallard said he had requested Coalition protection. Violence between the two communities had become a common occurrence. The Turkmen are the largest minority in Iraq after the Kurds; they claim to constitute

3 million of Iraq's 25 million people. In Kirkuk the Turkmen claim, based on a 1957 census, that 350,000 Turkmen live in the city and the surrounding villages. 'The highest percentage of the population here in Kirkuk is Arab and Turkmen. But here there are two occupations – one from the Kurd and one from the US. If they insist on making this kind of democracy, they will be sorry,' he said. 'My opinion in the name of the Turkmen is that since 1991 the US support and secure the Kurds. They give protection and the Kurds assist them.' He said that now the Peshmerga and the Kurdish-dominated police force were the twin powers in Kirkuk. 'We are afraid, everybody is afraid. On the 19th of this month [March] the car of Mr Safee [a well-known local Turkmen] was attacked with guns. The driver was injured. All the members here are afraid, as this is very common. The Kurds attack the Turkmen even with the Americans in the street.' He said his organisation had appealed to Bush and Bremer and that it wanted to get organisations like the UN and Human Rights Watch involved.

According to Tallard, what was going on was quite simple: the Kurds wanted to control Kirkuk so that they could control the surrounding oil fields. 'When the war ended, the Peshmerga entered the city and burned all the government buildings, including all the records of the population,' so that they could claim that Kirkuk was a predominantly Kurdish town. The US soldiers avoided Kirkuk and took control of the oil fields outside the town. The Kurds 'liberated' Kirkuk, a process that, according to the Turkmen, involved looting, burning and killing. He believed the idea had been to drive away the Arabs and the Turkmen in order to take over their property. He said many Arabs had left, but the Turkmen, with nowhere to go, had stayed. 'The Kurds will raise the population to make Kirkuk a Kurdish city. They are pushing the Kurdish people to get into Kirkuk so in a year's time they will win the election.'

When I asked him what he thought the Kurds wanted, his reply echoed what ordinary Kurds themselves would say to me, although it was at odds with what their leaders were saying in the Governing Council in Baghdad, 'One hundred per cent they still want independence in the future. In the future this kind of country will appear, as it serves American goals. Just like Israel.' I asked about a Turkmen representative on the Governing Council, Mrs Songul, but Tallard was disparaging. 'She was working as a translator with the US. The Turkmen people are not represented by this woman. She came here many times. She asked to assist in the front. We refused. She is different from us. She came with the US.' He talked for a while longer, asking me why the press was not interested in the problems of the Turkmen. I didn't know what to say. He repeated the familiar Iraqi refrain: 'The Americans offer freedom, democracy, but there is no freedom. It is turned around 180 degrees. There is no democracy here.'

\*

At the central police station, while I waited for the commander-in-chief, Captain Yadagr Shabdullah outlined the situation in Kirkuk. He was a Kurd originally from Kirkuk and his own history gave the other side of the story. He had arrived back in Kirkuk on the 'day of liberty', 10 April 2003, and immediately started work as a police officer. He had joined the Iraqi police in 1986 but had spent the period between 1991 and 2003 in Sulaimaniya. He was one of 3000 police officers who received training with the Coalition, 'preparing for this day of liberation', and they had entered Kirkuk four days before the Coalition forces. He said they seized the old police stations, which had been looted by the time they reached them, and proceeded to get to work establishing order. For the first three months, he said, all members of the 3000-strong police force were Kurds, but the percentages were now 47 per cent Kurd, 30 per cent Arab, 17 per cent Turkmen and some Christians, which he said reflected the ethnic mix of Kirkuk. 'We left our salaries in Kurdistan to make Iraq safe,' he said. 'We left Sulaimaniya and we came here for suffering. For ten years we were away from our city [Kirkuk].' He said initially there was looting by the local people, but no killing except in some of the villages. In July they had disarmed the population. 'No one in Kirkuk was allowed to carry a weapon. Not even in their car.' He said they used the confiscated weapons to arm their police force while the Americans destroyed those they seized. The Peshmerga had been forced to leave after a few weeks in order to protect the people and prevent fighting. 'We were controlling the revenge. Nobody was killed in the liberation of Kirkuk except maybe a few small incidents between families.'

Until December 2003, he said, Kirkuk was the safest city in Iraq. Then the bombings started. The first one was near the TV station that broadcast local programs in Kurdish; then the offices of the Kurdish and Turkmen political parties were targeted. Then a police station, killing seven police and wounding thirty-five on 23 February. Then came the attacks on police cars and security guards from the oil fields. By late March 2004, these attacks were occurring almost every day.

He speculated as to the source of the violence. He dismissed the possibility that supporters of Saddam or al-Qaeda were responsible. He dismissed Ansar al-Islam, the Kurdish Islamic group that was routed and fled across the border to Iran in the course of the war. He believed the culprits were groups in Kirkuk who opposed the peace. 'They are following a country nearby,' by which he meant Iran.

Captain Shabdullah said that the raid on the Turkmen National Front office was not carried out by the police and he didn't know who was responsible. As we talked, the local television station in the corner was showing a nightly staple: Kurdish lessons for the mixed population of Kirkuk.

Still waiting for the commissioner, we were taken to see the new Joint Operations Room. Shabdullah was very proud of it. There were computers, phones, radios and a large wide-screen TV and extensive maps of Kirkuk city and the surrounding areas on the walls. While the captain was showing us around, they received a call that three motorists had just been shot and killed by the US guards at the air base outside of town. These guards had been responding to three mortar shells fired on the base. He said there was no need for police involvement in this incident, and they contented themselves with circling the area in the report on one of the maps on the wall. The maps had clusters of red pins around certain areas of town to indicate the pattern of attacks on police. These were mostly just outside the town along the highways and in a small area in the downtown part of the city and around a certain bridge. The air base was also covered in small pins which denoted explosions and seven rocket attacks. About twenty-six police had been killed in the last six months and sixty-four injured. The staff entered into a long discussion about numbers injured, with a few of them gradually remembering names of officers they had forgotten at first. The attacks on the police and the US troops in Kirkuk were almost routine now, and the police would regularly find a pickup truck with a mortar abandoned in the back or an artillery shell in an abandoned car that was waiting to go off.

The police commander for Kirkuk, General Shirko Shahed, finally arrived. He started by telling me that even though he was a Kurd, his family had been in Kirkuk since the mid-nineteenth century. He said the problems in Kirkuk were due to foreign interference. The problem was the open borders, but didn't all countries in the world have terrorist problems, like in Spain, he asked. I pointed out that Spain didn't have bombs planted every day and armed men regularly attacking police. 'This kind of killing is very common everywhere. With our limited ability we are controlling the situation. We spend sixteen hours a day on duty,' he replied. He said that after six years the situation would normalise in Iraq, which was not such a long time considering how long his people had suffered. He said the problem in Kirkuk was that people did not want to call the police if there was trouble, and that although the police had taken away many of the guns, there were still knives. He was trying to play down the problems and felt that Kirkuk had an unjustifiably bad reputation. He admitted, though, that more and more attacks were directed against the police. As for the attacks on the oil facilities, well that was not his jurisdiction. It was late, around 9 p.m.; the commander received a call he said was from his wife and excused himself. The captain led us out through the coiled wire barricades to the now-deserted street. There were no cars on the road, and back at the small hotel I could hear shooting from the direction of the air base, but nobody seemed to be taking any notice as a small knot of men gazed at the television in the lobby. It was a kind of game show in Kurdish, and only a few of them understood it as the hotel was owned and run by a Turkmen, but still it was the only thing to watch.

\*

We headed up past the burning columns of flame the next day. We were on our way to Sulaimaniya, the PUK-controlled capital of Kurdistan, and it felt good to be away from Kirkuk. In Kirkuk the violence had many sources. It could be the Kurdish administration attacking the local Arabs or Turkmen. It could be local Arabs attacking the police. It could be Iraqi insurgents attacking the Americans or the oil pipelines. Or, at the bottom of the list, it could be foreign or foreign-backed militants trying to stir up the ethnic tensions that the Coalition denied existed.

For a few kilometres past the oil fields we saw signs of the previous year's fighting: a few abandoned and destroyed old Soviet tanks, a couple of deserted Iraqi army bases and, at the turn-off to Sulaimaniya, an abandoned tank painted in the blue, white and gold colours of the Kurds and a sign welcoming us to Kurdistan. The country after that was green and mountainous. The villages we drove through seemed almost deserted. Salah said that was because the people had been forced by their leadership to move down to Kirkuk. I was starting to doubt his interpretation of things. A Sunni from Baghdad, he had been up here last in the late 1970s, and he was gradually revealing an ingrained racism and disdain of the Kurds. He made a few jokes along the lines of Irish jokes, in which Kurds took the place of the clueless Irish.

After another hill, we came to the last well-established checkpoint before Sulaimaniya. It was built like a toll-way, or an international border crossing, which effectively it was. After this point there were no Arabs or Turkmen and barely any Coalition forces. The Kurds ran and policed it. It was their country and they wanted to keep the problems of Iraq locked out. All traffic was stopped and searched, and passports and documents had to be produced. Salah was quite brusquely marched away to the guardhouse while I was left to explain as best as I could that I was an Australian journalist and he was with me. An officer was summoned who asked me some very strange questions about Australia, including the performance of the Australian soccer team, about which I knew nothing. I explained that where I came from we followed another code of football, which seemed suspicious to him. It was only when I named the Australian journalist who had been killed in Kurdistan the previous year that the officer smiled and said I was very welcome. He apologised and said they had to be very careful. Salah was summoned and we were permitted to continue through the hills to Sulaimaniya where bus-loads of young Kurdish conscripts in dark uniforms shouted and waved at the villagers, who waved back, as we followed them into town.

Sulaimaniya is surrounded by hills and within sight of mountains which even in late March were still covered in snow. Driving into the crowded, narrow old streets was like returning to Europe by contrast with the flat, dusty, half-destroyed and deserted towns of Iraq. There were cafés and bars and shops selling jeans. I could see a shop selling books and newspapers in English. The pavement was crowded with people in Western-style clothes and women wearing make-up, without their heads covered. There were even shops with Britney Spears CDs and computers and mobile phones for sale (admittedly old ones). My first impulse was to get out of the car, leaving Salah and his increasingly apparent nervousness, and buy a newspaper, order a coffee and sit outside on the pavement and watch the people walk past, just as you might do in any Western city.

In my mind, Iraq seemed to divide into dissimilar zones. The south of Iraq, with its black-shrouded, rarely seen women and its dusty streets where the only decoration was massive billboards of Shiite clerics, was looking outward to Iran. The centre of the country seemed obsessed with its tortured past, its landscape one of broken remnants of the old regime: destroyed statues and shot-up pictures of Saddam and bomb-shattered public buildings. These sat alongside the ever-present Coalition razor wire, blast walls and sandbagged checkpoints that signified a new war against the outside world.

But here in Kurdistan they were looking to Europe and identifying and shaping their own culture around the culture of Western Europe. They were striving to be modern, which meant shopping and strolling on a

Sunday morning dressed in fashionable clothes, drinking coffee and eating outdoors and socialising. To a Westerner it was refreshing, but almost without realising what I was doing I checked myself. I couldn't help but notice what a perfect target these well-dressed people crowded onto these narrow sidewalks would be for a well-placed car bomb or suicide bomber. I looked around nervously for signs of police or soldiers.

It was about this time, stuck in the narrow streets, that the car started to stall ominously. We made it back to the main road and Salah tinkered with the engine while I went into a building with familiar golden arches. But it wasn't McDonalds, it was a local Kurdish copy called McDonnells, and although it had the same décor the menus looked as if they had been stolen from a fast-food shop in Turkey. The picture next to the cash register showed a smiling American officer with his arm around the owner. I ordered a Coke and a burger and fries and waited, excited to be eating something other than kebabs and greasy chicken. Salah came in stressed and sweating. He didn't know what was wrong with the car. He tried to order tea in Arabic, and the restaurant staff laughed at him. He bought a Coke instead and joined me. He was worried about the car and wanted to go back to Kirkuk. I told him we had to see some people first.

The main headquarters of the PUK was closed for the holidays. The men guarding it wore the traditional baggy-trousered uniform of the Peshmerga. They told us that they hadn't yet joined the army or police force like most of their comrades and were waiting re-assignment. For the time being they were guarding the headquarters. Bored, they invited us into the house next door for some tea, where five of them were living in the small front room. We sat down on the thin mats that were their beds, their clothes and weapons hanging on hooks on the walls around us. The oldest man started to speak. He had been in the Peshmerga for about thirty years, he said. They had fought briefly with the Iraqi Army in the Iran–Iraq war, and then with Iran. In 1996, when Turkey moved into the north, they fought its troops. They had to keep moving all the time. After the first Gulf War in 1991, they got Saddam out of the north, but then things were hard. Saddam came back and briefly took Sulaimaniya and they were forced into the hills. In 1991, he said, they captured Erbil, Sulaimaniya, Dohuk and Kirkuk, but then Saddam returned again. He said they had managed to keep Sulaimaniya after the no-fly zone was imposed. In 2003, they mainly fought Ansar al-Islam near the border with Iran, capturing some foreigners from Pakistan, Syria and Iran. He was old and hadn't seen his wife and two children since 1997. That was why he hadn't joined the police or the new army. He could neither read nor write – there had never been any time, they were always moving around. The only thing he wanted now was for the US forces to stay. But still he was happy, he said. He had liberated his people.

He pointed to the young man who was sitting with us. 'This young man here, he has nothing. He says he will work for free for two years if you take him to Europe.' The others were laughing, but the lad was deadly serious and nodded eagerly at us. He told us that he had left Kirkuk in 1997, when they had tried to make him join the Fedayeen Saddam. His brother was forced to join and was killed. He had not gone to school and had lived on the streets for a while before running away and joining the Peshmerga. 'All I know is that,' he said, pointing to his AK47 hanging on the wall. He was a good-looking boy, with sharp, confident movements, and he raised a laugh from everyone when he spoke. The older men indulged him. He pointed to my notebook: 'You are very lucky you can read and you are writing. I tried the school, but I have no time. I tried to escape to Turkey and to Greece and Europe, but the Turkish police they catch me.' The older man laughed at him and said that two-thirds of the young men in this area were now in Europe. 'All the young men from the Peshmerga have tried to go to Turkey.' Now, he said, some of them were thinking of staying in Sulaimaniya and were even getting married.

The older man had cousins in Finland and America. 'When we compare the situation in Europe and America with our cousins, we feel sorry for our situation. [Our cousins have] small jobs like selling ice cream [but] when they get back they get a car, buy a house, get an education. For me it is too late. I am married. I won't go now. We were born again when Saddam was gone. I was always ready to escape across the border, but now I stay.'

The young man was another story. Over and over he asked if I could take him with me. He didn't have a passport, and the older men kept telling him to wait at least until he had that. 'I am very tired of waiting. I want to go now,' he said. I tried to imagine this good-looking street tough with no language other than Kurdish and Arabic, no passport and no money sneaking around Europe. Perhaps he could find some manual work if he kept his head down and learnt a language. He could probably pass as Greek or southern Italian. But his nature seemed too exuberant and aggressive for this. There would be a fight or he'd be caught stealing. He didn't look the type to work hard for small sums of money when surrounded by the affluence of Western Europe. But here he was stuck living with these old men who had spent their lives fighting and were still at the bottom of their society, who were tired and wanted only to be released from duty but didn't really have lives to go back to. All he had were a couple of dirty shirts and an AK47. I wasn't going to lie to him and told him that he would probably end up in jail again if he tried to cross the border illegally. But he didn't care – anything was preferable to this, and he was tired of waiting. He was already twenty, he said. That was why he hadn't joined the army or the police and he was still in the Peshmerga, an unwanted relic that the Coalition were trying to disband. There were thousands like him who wanted nothing other than to get away from Kurdistan. They had done nothing but fight or be ready to fight and now they were no longer needed; it was the exiles coming back with the money who were able to enjoy the relative peace.

I had been told a huge revival in Kurdish culture was under way, and had planned to see some of this. There were societies of authors, new universities, new histories of the Kurdish nation being written, music, art – all the things that had been crushed by years of repression were now flowering. At least that was what I had been told. But being a national holiday and a Sunday, the offices were closed. The car was also fading fast. It stalled continually until the battery went dead from so many restarts. Police moved us on but offered no assistance because Salah could only speak Arabic and many of the younger people either didn't speak it or refused to. Finally we found a mechanic who got the car going again, but then, just as it grew dark, it stalled once more and this time we were surrounded by a pack of idle young men who reeked of the clear spirit raki. They began to taunt Salah and call him 'Mukhabarat' (Saddam's secret police). It was ugly and we eventually push-started the car and got out of there. The atmosphere was much the same when we went out to eat, and we wolfed down our food to get away from the young men making anti-Arab comments at the next table. You couldn't blame them. They had just won their independence and many horrible things had been done to them. Almost everyone in Kurdistan had lost a family member during the time of Saddam, and almost everyone had been a refugee at some stage or another in the past thirty years. It had looked like a refreshingly free place when we arrived, but as we walked back to the hotel, groups of young men yelled and smashed bottles in our direction. There had been no bombing to that point in Sulaimaniya, and the hotel owner told me he was proud of the town's safety. For me it probably was the safest city in Iraq, but for Salah it was enemy territory, and already, despite what the leaders were saying, a different country.

\*

We crawled back to Kirkuk the next morning with the car seemingly now running on one cylinder. I had organised an interview with the US Army representative, and Salah dropped me by the concrete barriers and chugged off to find a mechanic. The US soldiers on the gate had recently arrived from their base in Hawaii and laughed at the sorry state of the car. Major Samuel Schubert was eating a cheeseburger and offered me a Diet Coke when he finally arrived. The government building in which I'd been waiting was like a fortress; armed civilian contractors with small machine-guns and small earpieces stood at the top of the stairwell and patrolled the corridors. In the thirty minutes it took for the Major to arrive, they checked my ID six times.

'Look, the crime rate here is less than San Jose, California,' he said when I asked him about the problems. Two police officers had been killed and two wounded the day before at a drive-by shooting at a checkpoint, but aside from the mortars on the base (he didn't know anything about the civilian casualties reported by the police) there had only been one major VBIED in the two months since his arrival.

He said he didn't know who had looted the town and the shootings at the demonstrations were a simple mistake. 'Hell, they have demonstrations all the time here. It is a sign of democracy.' One of his jobs was re-allocating the government buildings, which he said was creating tensions between the different communities. On the topic of the influx of Kurds into Kirkuk, he said, 'It's a free country. They can live wherever they like. It's a long-term strategy to move in and get the votes. When they take someone else's property, that is when we have to intervene.' When I asked him about the guard on the Turkmen office, he just looked at me and said, 'What did they tell you?' He saw foreigners as his major problem. 'We are concerned with people coming from Iran. Bad guys, not the good guys. Any terrorist organisation, al-Qaeda, Ansar al-Islam, offshoots of Ansar al-Islam. They could be the real thing or they could be just cowboys. We investigate causes and effects, but I can't give you that information even if I had it.' He said they investigated every foreign national who came through, and sometimes they brought them in for questioning.

I asked how many they had arrested and he said this information was classified. I asked how many troops they had there and he said that too was classified. He said Kirkuk was a fine example of a multi-ethnic city that was working.

# LAST DAYS

On the slow drive back to Baghdad we stopped to photograph a roadblock that was manned by ICDC troops.
The Coalition had been releasing frequent statements
that such tasks were now being handed over to Iraqis.
When we asked to take their picture, the troops all gladly
lined up with their backs to the passing traffic they were
supposed to be watching. In the resulting photo, they
were smiling at the camera and looked a little like a
football team. One of the soldiers grabbed my camera
and gestured to me to join the others. Another thrust an
AK47 in my hands and I took care not to touch the trigger, thinking that I might accidentally set it off. There
was a lot of laughing and backslapping, and as we talked
they complained that unlike the Coalition troops they
had no body armour and only had AK47s and one light
machine-gun whereas the insurgents had RPGs. As it
began to grow dark, we headed off. The troops were
bored and wandered back to their post on top of a pile

of dirt-filled blast bags. Less than an hour later the post was attacked and one ICDC soldier killed in a gun battle that didn't end until US troops arrived. One US soldier was killed and one wounded, and three rebels were killed before they retreated.

We didn't know about that and continued on through the flat, darkening desert, comfortable in the anonymity of Salah's chugging and by now filthy car, which thankfully kept running even in Baghdad's stop-start traffic. We were congratulating ourselves that we had made it back when we pulled up at the *Time* house. I was still laughing as I walked in through the gate, until Stephan Faris walked up to me and said, 'Omar was shot dead outside the house this morning on his way here. He is not dead yet, but they shot him in the head and the chest. We are evacuating the house now.' Omar was one of the permanent translators employed by *Time*, a former engineer who had lived and studied in England. He had no enemies, he had been shot because he worked for foreigners. The location of the shooting meant that his killers knew about the house full of Western journalists and their Iraqi helpers. It was like a slap in the face. We had been living, we thought, anonymously in the suburbs among ordinary Iraqis, away from the guns, tanks, razor wire and hovering helicopters of the other hotels that Iraqis were too afraid to approach and which only reinforced the distance between them and us and fed the paranoia of the Westerners staying there. Two weeks before, a translator for *Voice of America* radio had been killed in a similar attack, and then a *Washington Post* translator's house had been destroyed by a bomb. Now it was our turn, and we had to run like the rest of them back to the Coalition-protected hotels, and Omar, who had spent most of his time at the house organising interviews and giving endless advice to the frequently rotated journalists, was lying in hospital dying.

The guard at the front told Salah the news before driving away. Salah had been a good friend of Omar's and he was almost in tears as he drove me into town with my bags. I managed to get a room at the Al-Fanar and briefly went and saw the *Time* translators, drivers and even their cook being frisked and all their luggage searched as they negotiated the checkpoint to the Palestine Hotel opposite. Everybody seemed in shock. The implication of the assassination was that the *Time* workers were all being watched, and so it wasn't safe for anyone to go home.

Omar died the following night at the American hospital in the Green Zone. His wounds were so extensive that nothing could be done for him. The first I knew of it was when Salah called me. He was crying, they were already burying him, he was with his family. I could hear weeping in the background. He was worried that I would be without a car. I was amazed he was concerned about me at the funeral of his good friend. I said it was okay, my work wasn't that important.

Salah came around later that day and took me to Omar's family home. It was the custom for the bereaved to gather for three days after a death and pray. We sat for a while. It was terribly sad. The house was on a small suburban street and the yard was filled with people on chairs quietly praying, including all of the guards and drivers and translators from the *Time* house. Omar was a highly educated, middle-class man in his mid-forties. I was told later that the only reason he had returned to Iraq after studying engineering in England was because the authorities threatened his brother and also threatened to confiscate the family land if he did not return. He had liked England and his English was perfect. He would mock my Australian accent and often ask about emigrating to Australia or New Zealand and joke that I would not let him stay in my house in Australia for as long as I had stayed in theirs in Baghdad. Omar had tried to talk me out of going to Falluja as he considered it too dangerous, but had then organised for me to go with the right people when I insisted. He was one of the few translators and drivers who never carried a weapon.

During the next few days I did some writing and tried to decide whether to stay or leave Iraq. I visited the *Time* reporters at the Palestine, but they had their own problems. Some of the translators had been threatened in their homes, and in one case they had needed to organise armed men to retrieve one from his house after he had hidden from men who were looking for him. Salah told me that after Omar was shot, locals told him that men had come around asking questions about whether he had died or not; he believed these were the same men who had shot him.

It was profoundly unsettling for them to know that they had been watched and earmarked for death for working with foreigners. Salah took it in his stride, saying, 'It is just like being in the army this job. You just accept death is part of getting to the truth.' His brother was more morose. He had been a friend of Omar's since high school. He had been conscripted and fought in the Iran war as a tank commander while Omar went to England, then worked for the INA, the Iraqi news agency. One journalist had refused to work with Salah's brother, saying he was an unreconstructed Baathist. For my part, I thought he was terminally depressed. While Salah's car was being repaired, his brother offered to drive me around. Once, as we drove past a demonstration of former Ministry of Information employees, he said, 'In Iraq you have to do nothing. Me, I haven't worked for a year for any papers or magazines. What is there to tell the people? They live it every day. Maybe for you American journalists or the Australian people, maybe they want to know, but for us ...' He trailed off. Omar's death had upset him deeply and he viewed the entire situation with barely disguised contempt. 'Why go out? Everybody is jobless. Look around between eight and four during the day. There are people everywhere, doing nothing, making trouble, killing people.'

One night I visited Stephan at the Palestine and he invited me to a poker night at the *Washington Post* room in the Sheraton. The room resembled a bunker set up for a siege or else a bachelor's paradise. Cartons of beer were stacked along one wall, and bottled water and food and equipment were scattered everywhere. Around the table were correspondents from the *Washington Post*, the *New Yorker*, Stephan from *Time* and two young Americans who held aid-related jobs in the Green Zone. They were in their twenties and as far as they were concerned, 'Iraq rocked' and 'Iraqis rocked.' Perhaps they were rich kids just out of college who had picked up work in Iraq. Perhaps they were very good spooks with a dumb-and-dumber cover. I realised I didn't really care: they brought some cheer to an otherwise grim gathering and made me remember that there was actually a world outside this small compound.

Meanwhile the Marine operation had begun in Falluja. The retreat of December 2003 to a base outside town had been replaced by a bloody-minded insistence on moving the troops back in. During the first three days of the operation, the Marines lost five of their own. No one was keeping track of Iraqi deaths.

On another night, restless and unable to sleep in the Al-Fanar, I decided to go for a walk to the Sheraton. The US soldiers on the gate were as uncommunicative as ever, and the foyer was empty. I pressed the lift button to the 'rooftop bar', thinking it would be great if there was such a thing. The doors opened to a short Nepalese man carrying a submachine-gun and wearing blue body armour. I said *Namaste* and asked for the bar and he walked me to a door and opened it. There it was, a bar with pool tables, music and people seated around a bar with a 360-degree view of the Baghdad skyline. I couldn't believe it.

It didn't last. Soon I realised that everyone there was wearing bits and pieces of military gear and a sniper's rifle was sitting on the bar. The American woman behind the bar had just opened my cold Heineken when the man next to me said, 'Who the hell are you and how the hell did you get in here?' I explained that I was an Australian journalist who wanted a drink. He angrily sent someone out to reprimand the Nepalese and said, 'OK my friend, you can stay for one beer, but all I can talk to you about is sports. Ain't you Australians into sports? I love to watch that football of yours on the pay-per-view back home.' So I managed to stay for three. They were contractors, securing the hotel, covering all the roads and the surrounding buildings with their night-vision-equipped sniper rifles. Eventually they asked me what it was like outside; they weren't allowed to leave the hotel perimeter and had been there for months without once setting foot in Baghdad. They had everything they needed up there. Even their meals were brought up to them. They laughed and said it was an easy way to spend their six-month contract, but wouldn't tell me how much they were being paid. When I left, they told me never to consider coming back up.

The next morning, while I was breakfasting at the Al-Fanar, a terrific boom shook the windows. The only other diner was a Japanese journalist and we raced down-stairs to see what it was. One of the drivers downstairs said it was an IED nearby, in Abu Nawas Street. He was right, and the Japanese journalist left with him. The IED had killed four Iraqis working as translators or body-guards for the CPA when it blew up as their car was going past. The insurgents had probably believed them to be contractors.

On that day, my last in Baghdad, Salah's brother took me to a fish restaurant run by a friend of his. He seemed to be as depressed as Salah's brother. He gave me a Pepsi and told me to leave Iraq. 'We will start killing foreign-ers in the street soon.' The open-air restaurant had huge dirty tanks of gawking river fish and a broken-down, grimy look. I drank my Pepsi and the owner refused to take my money.

We drove out to Camp Victory at Baghdad Airport to interview members of the tiny Australian contingent in Iraq. Salah's brother ignored the signs to slow down at the checkpoint and instead drove straight up to it. Instantly guns were pointed at us from all directions. A huge black American sergeant walked up slowly with a machine-gun levelled at the car while I jumped out the door yelling not to shoot, I was a journalist. 'What the fuck are you doing? Do you want to get yourself killed?' he screamed, and I started to believe that maybe Salah's brother did.

After writing a last piece on the Australian contin-gent until late in the night, I drank some whisky and my head had barely hit the pillow when the car arrived to take me to Jordan. There had been some fighting near Falluja with the Marines; we had to leave now, my driver said, it would be too dangerous later. We left and I fell asleep across the comfortable back-seat of the GMC. I didn't wake until we were past Ramadi in the west and there were no more towns between us and the Jordanian border.

*

Two days later, in transit to Australia passing through Singapore airport, I picked up a copy of the *Straits Times*. There was a picture of the destroyed car of the four American 'contractors' who had been ambushed and killed in the main street of Falluja. The report described how the ecstatic crowd had paraded their bodies around the town and chanted slogans, including 'There is no God but God and America is the enemy of God'. Just like the ones I had seen written on walls there and elsewhere in Iraq. The bodies had been dangled from a bridge and the entire debacle had been filmed and photographed.

Back in Australia the next day and unable to sleep, I watched family members of the victims describe them as heroes to the US *Today* show. One of them, Scott Helveston, had been a physical instructor and stunt man in Hollywood. The pictures showed a brawny, perfectly built muscle-man, who had been Demi Moore's personal trainer for *GI Jane*, a film about a female soldier in the

US Army. He went to Iraq for the challenge and the money, they said on the voiceover, although Hollywood had paid him well. I wondered what he and his fellow security contractors were doing in Falluja in the middle of a Marines operation. The Iraqis who killed them had taken them for CIA agents, with their blue body armour, civilian clothes and assortment of high-powered weapons. Perhaps they were. And they would have been shooting civilian Iraqis with those weapons. What were they doing there? Nobody asked that, and because their grisly deaths were recorded it was an outrage. A barbaric act against America. The Marines vowed revenge and at least a thousand Iraqis in Falluja would die over the next two weeks.

In the next few days the Shiite followers of Moqutada al-Sadr began fighting Coalition troops. The Coalition had banned their newspaper *Al Hawza* on 28 March. The al-Sadr people responded by declaring they would fight the Coalition, and the Coalition responded by issuing an arrest warrant for their leader. The fighting spread to the holy cities of Karbala and Najaf. As the Marines intensified their attack on Falluja, laying siege to the city and blocking all traffic in and out while attacking the area with helicopters, fighter planes, tanks and infantry, the kidnappings of foreigners began in earnest. Some were released, some were killed and one escaped.

Then in mid-April came the pictures of the abuse and torture by US soldiers of Iraqi detainees in the prison of Abu Ghraib. The moral authority of the US was gone, and it became common for those outside Iraq to begin finally to refer to the Coalition presence in Iraq as an occupation, not a liberation.